Hi Mom! Hi Dad!

101 cartoons for
New Parents
by Lynn Johnston

⁊⁊Meadowbrook
Distributed by Simon & Schuster
New York

Meadowbrook Press Edition
15th printing, February 1985

PRINTED IN THE UNITED STATES OF AMERICA
Library of Congress Number 77-82216

ISBN 0-915658-06-2

Copyright © 1977 by Lynn Johnston

Published by Meadowbrook, Inc., Deephaven,
MN 55391

BOOK TRADE DISTRIBUTION by Simon and
Schuster, a division of Simon & Schuster, Inc.,
1230 Avenue of the Americas, New York,
NY 10020
S & S Ordering #: 0-671-54482-9

THE FIRST YEAR OF LIFE

A tiny bundle of life is placed in your arms, and at first it's hard to believe that you are now a parent. The overwhelming feeling of responsibility for another life, the pride and joy in your "creation", but also the concomitant feelings of inadequacy in your new role, frequently surface during that first year.

Lynn Johnston, with humour and sensitivity, creates cartoons that depict the feelings and reactions of parents as they learn to respond to the needs of the growing child, to the reactions of in-laws and relatives, to the pressures of the mass media, the experts, and the child-rearing fads. As we chuckle at the captions, we are reminded of the incredible amount of hardship experienced by parents during the baby's first year—the loss of sleep, the feeling of helplessness when the baby cries and can't be comforted, and the new precautions we have to take as the baby acquires new competencies and skills, as he or she learns to reach and grasp objects, sit up, creep, and finally becomes upright and mobile.

The baby becomes a "real" personality and enriches the life of the family. The joy experienced by the parents makes the struggle well worthwhile. The recognition of this joy is captured in the last cartoon: "To think that before we had a baby, this was just the same old park!"

With a few deft strokes of her pen, Lynn Johnston shows us what the first year of life is like. Her delightfully subtle cartoons at once make the hardships of life with baby more bearable.

— Mary Blum, Psychologist

7

8

hy is it that after
ne months, 14 hours
bor, an episiotomy
nd hemorrhoids...
still find it hard to
elieve you're really
ere!
LYNN

10

11

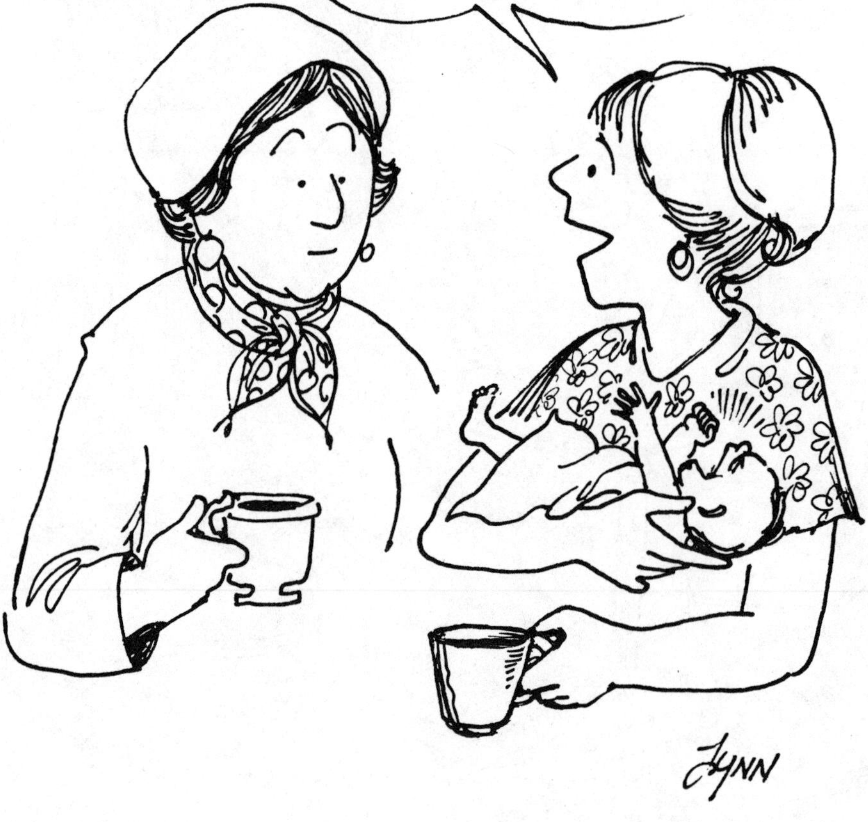
She's really quite pretty when she's sleeping...
LYNN

14

15

16

17

19

I haven't seen myself without hair there since I was twelve....
LYNN

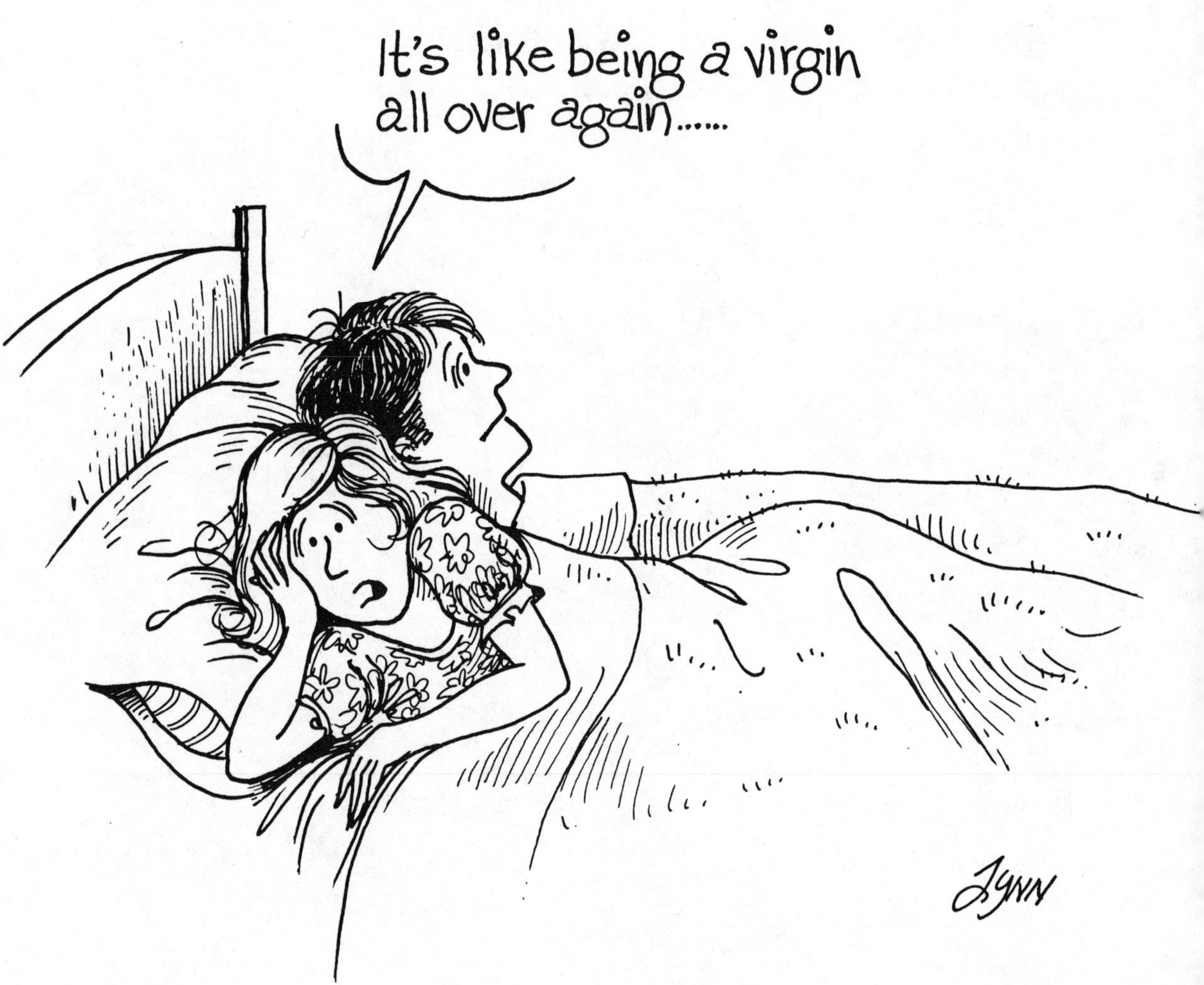
It's like being a virgin all over again......
LYNN

24

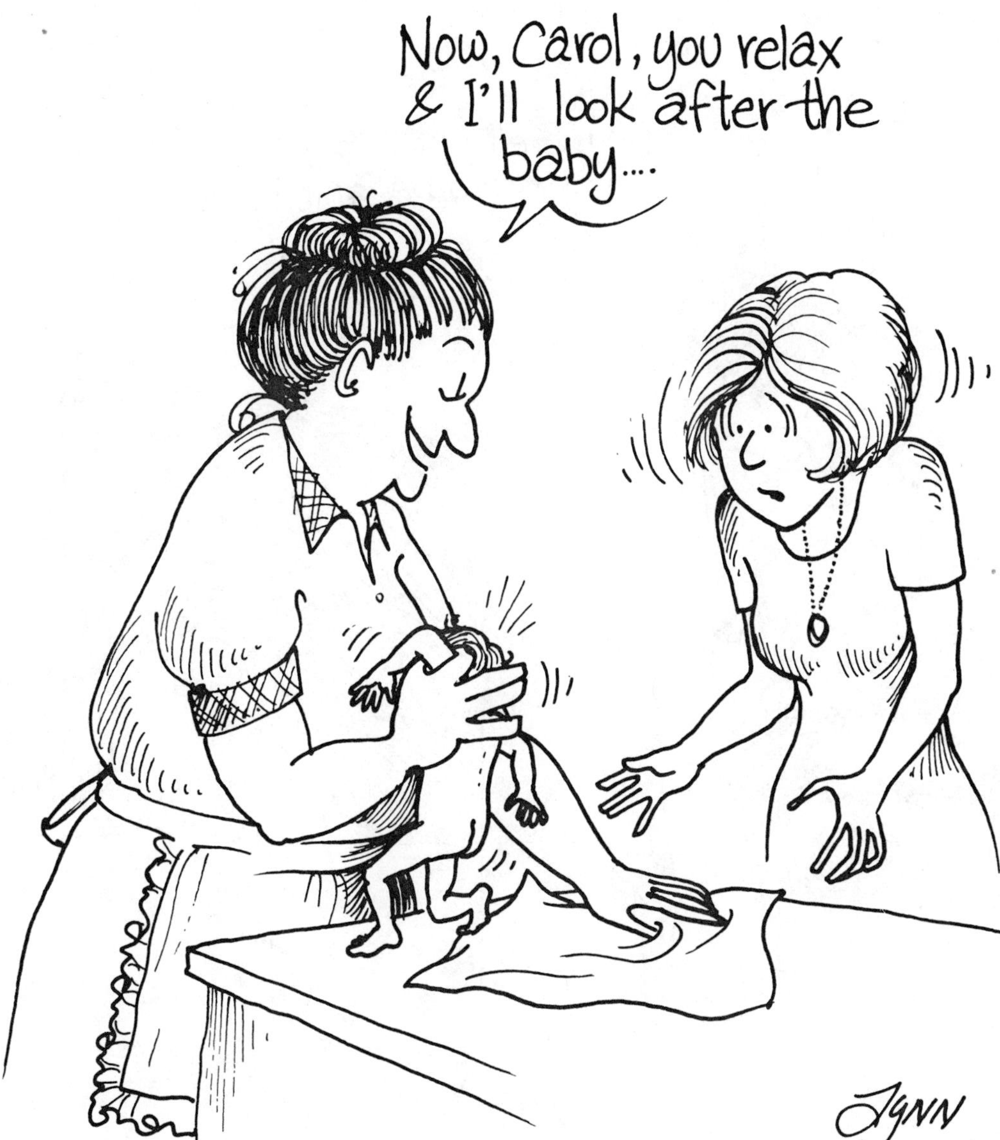
Now, Carol, you relax & I'll look after the baby....
LYNN

Hey, Dad, where's this soft spot everyone's talking about?
SUNDAY
LYNN

28

29

30

33

34

36

I've tried feeding and rocking...and singing...and burping and bathing and pleading...and walking and shouting and whispering and... changing... and....

38

ar Mom, you ask if we enjoy parenthood. Well,
er 3 weeks of getting used to the situation,
can safely say ~~that we are already~~ that
~~ings are that the baby is~~ Mom, can you
ake it out here?

Lynn

39

41

43

44

47

49

51

52

53

55

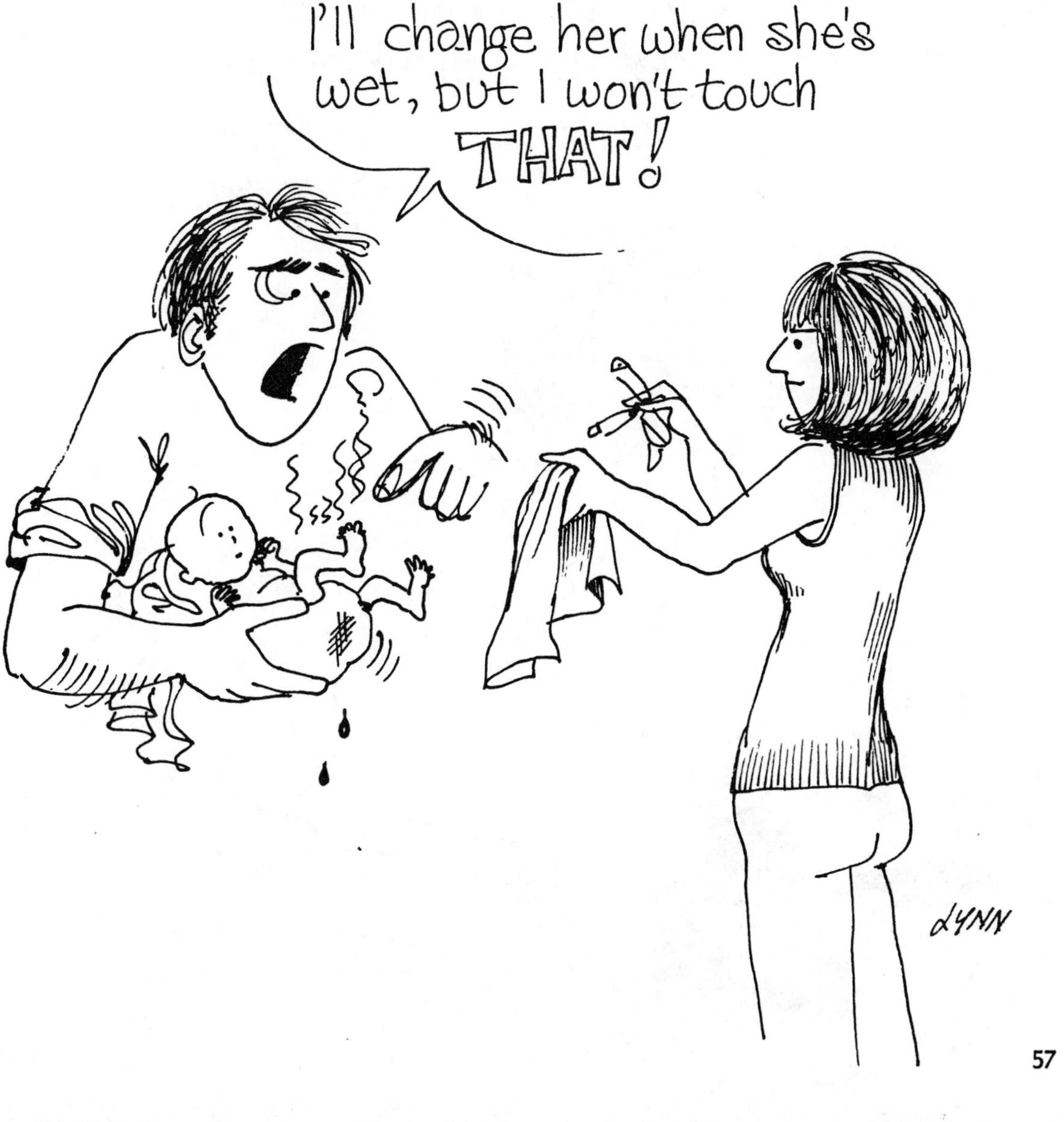
I'll change her when she's wet, but I won't touch THAT!
LYNN

58

60

61

63

65

69

70

71

72

...ela? you were right!
...hrew out all the teething
...cuits..... This
...ld be a new
...e for
...K BONE!

75

Wow! if finding his fingers makes him THIS happy-wait'll he discove
ORIFICES!!
LYNN

79

82

83

86

91

93

94

95

LYNN

97

99

101

It's nice to be needed.

104

106

Meet Lynn Johnston

Lynn Johnston is the best-selling female cartoonist in North America with good reason. She draws much of her material from close observation of her family—Aaron, Katie, and husband Roderick, a "flying dentist" whose practice is based in Lynn Lake (no relation), 800 miles north of Winnipeg, Manitoba. Her deft, humorous depictions of life with kids have provided her with material for three books, published by Meadowbrook, and now she has a family comic strip, "For Better or For Worse" running in newspapers throughout North America.

& Her Books:

Parenting Books

Our Baby's First Year

A Baby Record Calendar

A nursery calendar with 13 undated months for recording "big events" of baby's first year. Each month features animal characters, and baby care and development tips. Photo album page and family tree, too! A great shower gift!

(S & S Ordering #: 54486-1) $7.95

Parents' Guide to Baby & Child Medical Care
by Terril H. Hart, M.D.

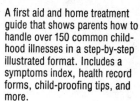

A first aid and home treatment guide that shows parents how to handle over 150 common childhood illnesses in a step-by-step illustrated format. Includes a symptoms index, health record forms, child-proofing tips, and more.

(S & S Ordering #: 54470-5) $7.95

Dear Babysitter

With Sitter's Handbook and Instruction Pad

DEAR BABYSITTER is really two sitter aids in one – a 50-page refillable instruction Pad plus a Sitters' Handbook of activities and emergency procedures – both securely bound in a sturdy washable hardcover binding.

(S & S Ordering #: 54477-2) $7.95

My First Years

A Keepsake Baby Record Book

A colorful, durable baby record book that offers a convenient way to record a baby's first five years. The beautiful padded cover, with a charming stitchery design, opens to reveal 32 four-color pages for recording everything from arrival day to kindergarten.

(S & S Ordering #: 54543-4) $10.95

Parenting Books

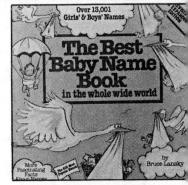

Hundreds of parent-tested ideas for the first five years. Includes topics such as baby care, feeding, self esteem and more.
Spiral bound.
(S & S Ordering #: 54487-X)
$5.95

The most popular baby book and tot food cookbook for new parents. Includes over 200 recipes and ideas.
Spiral bound.
(S & S Ordering #: 54480-2)
$5.95

A fully illustrated child care handbook that covers the first twelve months of life—when parents need help most! Includes step-by-step photos and illustrations.
(S & S Ordering #: 54497-7)
$5.95

The most complete, up-to-date, helpful, entertaining and gifty baby name book ever. Includes over 10,000 names.
(S & S Ordering #: 54463-2) $3.95

BREAK THE TAKE-OUT HABIT

Forget about opening cans, eating still another tuna sandwich, or heating up a TV dinner. For less than the cost of fast food, you can make fabulous meals at home that will please your tastebuds, your sense of style, and your pocketbook. Every recipe here is designed to provide hassle-free meals with quick, delicious results. Whether you're just learning to cook or are too busy to bother . . . whether you're a dieter, a big eater, a single person, a family member, or someone on a restricted diet, this simplified cookbook offers enough recipes and variations to take you through a whole year of great eating. It's for everyone who wants to eat like a gourmet without spending hours in the kitchen.

THE THREE-INGREDIENT COOKBOOK

SONDRA J. STANG, a native New Yorker, lives with her husband in St. Louis, where she raised her three children (now all adults and contributors to this cookbook). She has lived abroad for four years, cooking in kitchens in Germany and England and always looking out for the right three ingredients.

THE
THREE-INGREDIENT
COOKBOOK

WITH OTHER SIMPLE RECIPES

Sondra J. Stang

A PLUME BOOK

NEW AMERICAN LIBRARY

NEW YORK AND SCARBOROUGH, ONTARIO

PLUME TRADEMARK REG. U.S. PAT. OFF. AND FOREIGN COUNTRIES
REG. TRADEMARK—MARCA REGISTRADA
HECHO EN HARRISONBURG, VA., U.S.A.

SIGNET, SIGNET CLASSIC, MENTOR, PLUME, MERIDIAN
and NAL BOOKS are published *in the United States*
by New American Library, 1633 Broadway,
New York, New York 10019, *in Canada* by
The New American Library of Canada Limited,
81 Mack Avenue, Scarborough, Ontario M1L 1M8.

LIBRARY OF CONGRESS CATALOGING IN PUBLICATION DATA

Stang, Sondra J.
  The three-ingredient cookbook.

  Includes index.
  1. Cookery.   I. Title.
TX652.S656   1985   641.5   84–25491
ISBN 0–452–25666–6

First Printing, August, 1985

1 2 3 4 5 6 7 8 9

PRINTED IN THE UNITED STATES OF AMERICA

For my mother

I think everyone now has to learn to cook. . . .
W. H. AUDEN

Acknowledgments

I thank my children—David, Elizabeth, and Sam—who in their several capacities were the catalyst for this book, contributors to it, and testers of recipes. My husband, Richard Stang, while not a cook himself, has always been my greatest source of sensible advice both in and out of the kitchen.

I am indebted to my many friends who, excellent cooks all of them, read through the manuscript as critically and helpfully as possible. Miriam Munson helped me prepare the final manuscript, combing through the preliminary version carefully, instructing and enlightening me, clarifying the language, improving the recipes, overcoming difficulties, and contributing recipes of her own (while Rebecca waited, slept, or smiled). Joe Loewenstein made valuable suggestions at every stage of the manuscript, contributed recipes, read through the final version, questioned and challenged and sharpened my wits. With infinite patience, Rheba Symeonoglou and Judy and Laura Zwicker solved insoluble problems in the course of copyediting, and I am grateful for their considerable powers as cooks and careful observers of the changes that take place in food as it cooks.

I am particularly grateful to Judy Admussen, Janice Biala, Willard and Evvy Cobb, Mona Van Duyn, and Marion Steefel, whose enthusiasm for this book took the form of volunteering more and more material as I was writing. I thank Willard and Evvy Cobb and Martha Rudner for reading parts of the manuscript and testing recipes—correcting, improving, and clarifying in every instance. Lee Robins read part of the manuscript, and I am grateful for her suggestions.

I would like to acknowledge the part my cousin Laura Popenoe played as my collaborator at the inception of this book. Her presence hovers; her recipes are firmly in place. Michael Philips is responsible for discouraging the use of more than three ingredients in all cooking on general principles; I hope he will be forgiving wherever I've transgressed.

Eleanor Hochman and Elaine Pfefferblit, midwives to this enterprise, followed it with interest from its beginnings. Without them, three-ingredient cooking would have remained an idea rather than a cookbook.

Part of this book is the work of friends who, intrigued by its plan, offered me their very simplest and nicest recipes. In some way, in fact, the book is a sort of history of my friendships, beginning more than thirty years ago when I began to discover a community of spirits all eager to acquire—and divulge—recipes that were almost effortless—and a good deal more than just serviceable.

So I thank all the following people for their recipes, as well as suggestions, information, and encouragement. I am enormously grateful to them all: Marge and Solon Beinfeld; Jonathan Bishop; Anne Borchardt; Marge Cardwell; Stanley and Joan Elkin; Sondra Foa-Birkett; Ford Madox Ford; John Garganigo; Bill and Mary Gass; Sheila Gordon; Ellen Hamingson; Osman Janneh; David Kalstone; Bernard Kaminstein; Tom Kirk; Nancy Kollmar; Marie Kremer; Penny Kuhn; Susie Leff; Hannah Loewenhaupt; Allen Mandelbaum; James Merrill; Annelise Mertz; Maria Michaelides; Brenda Mindock; Mary Mottl; Dean Olsen; Mary Ann Rochette; Samudra; Judy Savoie; Dorla Schwarz; Miriam Selvansky; Edith Silver; Gail Smiley; Eleanor Smith; Sarah Steefel; Becky Tracy; Wally Tworkov; Jackie Wheeler; Phoebe Weil; Regina Zimmerman—and the butcher on Broadway and 111th Street (c. 1950), whose name I cannot recall.

I thank Stanley Demos of the Coach House Restaurant, Louisville, Kentucky, for French-Fried Sweet Potatoes and Wayne R. Johnson, Product Manager of Durkee Famous Foods for Zing Wings. And I am much obliged to Rita Malenczyk for her care and acuteness in supplying the index.

Finally, I salute Kay Drey, whose needs I have kept in mind; surely the busiest of all the people I know and for over twenty years a new cook, with this book she may or may not continue to call at six P.M. and ask what she should do with a pound of frozen ground beef.

CONTENTS

INTRODUCTION

This book is for people who need help in the kitchen:
- men and women setting up their own households
- college students who have left the dorms (and dorm food) and are living in apartments, trying to cook for themselves
- mothers and fathers caring for children after a day of work
- divorced men who feel the only meal they can prepare is breakfast
- experienced cooks who would like a holiday from more elaborate cooking
- would-be cooks intimidated by long recipes

In short, this book is for all people who are simply too inexperienced, too busy, or too tired to do more than the most minimal cooking, yet who like to eat well and with style.

This book is also intended for older people whose families are gone and who are perhaps living alone for the first time—people for whom money may be a problem, and while time may not be, they lack the energy or inclination to go to great trouble "just" for themselves. This collection of recipes, energy and time-saving, economical, and easy to use, is for them.

It is also for families with broken eating patterns, with husbands, wives, and children eating at different times. And for all the noncooks who must fend for themselves, it demonstrates that they don't *have* to eat bleakly; indeed, the simple and explicit directions will help them become cooks.

About the Recipes

Here then is a collection of extremely easy recipes containing a very limited number of ingredients and directions and reflecting a large number of shortcuts. Many of the recipes are simplified versions of more ambitious dishes; wherever possible, I have presented both the basic model and optional ways of adding to it or varying or refining it. Simple solutions are no less honorable than complicated ones, and my book is based on the belief that homemade fast food using fresh, natural, and, for the most part, inexpensive ingredients can be a pleasure to eat and a true alternative to the fast food empires. I suspect a good many people turn to fast food not because they particularly like what they get but because they think it's too much trouble to cook, or they don't know how and don't know how to begin to learn.

Most cookbooks, including those for beginners, offer too many recipes, too many choices, too much instruction, too much print, but perhaps worst of all, too many ingredients to assemble. The psychological effect of all this is, in most cases, to overwhelm, confuse, or discourage those who are wary of cooking in the first place.

I know a middle-aged man who subsists mostly on peanut butter sandwiches and hamburgers from McDonald's. Why didn't he try cooking for himself? I asked him. "Because when there are more than three ingredients and more than three steps, it's too much hassle," was his answer.

As I thought about his remark, it seemed more and more worth taking seriously. It struck me that the most useful thing I could do in a cookbook was to keep the scale of each recipe as small as possible and to suggest through the simplicity of the recipes that putting a good meal together *is* within the realm of possibility for people with marginal cooking skills or none at all.

This is why the book consists mainly of three-ingredient recipes. At the end of most of the sections I offer some four-ingredient recipes for those who may wish to move on, and hither and yon there are even some two-ingredient recipes.

These three or four ingredients do not include spices,

herbs, or other seasonings, which I list as part of a basic seasoning shelf (see pages 19–22 and the list on pages 246–252). By ingredients I mean the essential foods that go into the making of a dish. The seasonings, with all due respect to their powers and influence over a dish, are nevertheless secondary.

In the recipes, I list the ingredients separately from the seasonings because I have tried to imagine the point of view of a novice cook whose basic problem is simply to grasp the essentials of a recipe and *see* its basic contents, unencumbered by secondary details. I believe that the format I use makes it easy for the reader to take in the recipe.

Recipes should be read, reread, and really understood before the cook even begins to assemble the ingredients. Going through the entire recipe mentally makes the actual process more familiar and far less intimidating.

Each of the recipes in this book has only three steps. The directions vary, from a sequence of three absolutely simple, single steps to some that combine a series of related actions in each step (much as conventional cookbooks combine them in a single paragraph).

About the Ingredients

As a general rule, the recipes use fresh, raw, wholesome, and natural ingredients. While this is a book of shortcuts and simplifications, I cannot in good conscience recommend that anyone mix potato chips, tuna fish, and a can of cream of mushroom soup to make an acceptable dinner. The use of canned food is kept to a minimum—chicken or beef stock when there is no homemade stock, canned tomatoes, tomato sauce, tomato juice, tomato paste, canned beans, or occasionally canned fruit. The emphasis is on using raw materials that are in fact no more demanding than the directions on many cans or packages of "instant" prepared foods—those food "products" that taste no better than cardboard.

When a recipe in this book calls for frozen spinach, it is because the careful washing that fresh spinach requires to rid it of all sand may be a real deterrent to the readers for whom this book was written. Spinach is less damaged in the freezing process than most other vegetables, as are peas; since both frozen spinach and frozen peas tend to be of uniform quality, without the bitterness of some fresh spinach and the tastelessness of some fresh peas, I recommend them.

The question of chicken or beef stock is a difficult one. Ideally, all cooks should have a supply of homemade stock in small containers in the freezer (easy directions for preparing stock can be found in the Useful Techniques section, pages 276–277). The next best thing is canned stock although most brands tend to be oversalted; bouillon cubes are also over-salted, but they are handy and easy to store. Neither canned stock nor bouillon cubes can be described as delicious, but they are always available. Whenever possible, however, I recommend using homemade stock.

I am very much aware of the need for a prudent diet, using low-cholesterol foods as often as possible. I don't always succeed—cream, eggs, and cheese being some of the better things in this world. This is, of course, not a diet cookbook but a book written for very diverse readers. The recipes do call for relatively small amounts of oil, as often as possible for safflower or corn oil. Readers may, if they wish, substitute low-fat milk for cream, yogurt or buttermilk for sour cream, or low-cholesterol margarine for butter.

Olive oil seems to me the most delicious of all oils, and I suggest that readers buy the best quality they can, since the flavor of the oil greatly influences the final flavor of the dish in which it is used. This is true of canned tomatoes as well: the canned plum tomatoes from Italy are best, far better than the domestic cans, which contain preservatives and sugar. Fresh homegrown ripe tomatoes are better yet, but they are seasonal (the supermarket tomatoes sold all year around have very little flavor). Soup, sauce, or stew will gain immensely when good tomatoes are used—and at that the cost is still a good deal less than the cost of takeout food.

I have tried to keep to a minimum the number of pots and pans called for in cooking any dish, and there are enough one-pot or one-pan ideas for dinner to interest the weariest cook. Other practical matters shaped my choice of recipes.

What to do with a package of frozen hamburger meat? What to cook for an unexpected guest? What to cook for oneself when there is almost nothing on the kitchen shelf? The Index should be of help, "emergency food" being one of the listings.

Other Information

There is, in fact, a good deal of material at the back of the book that should not be overlooked. The section on Herbs and Spices (page 246) gives information about buying, storing, and using them. Since the same dish will seem different with different seasoning, readers are encouraged to consult these pages and try variations of their own. The Glossary of Cooking Terms (page 279) provides definitions of unfamiliar terms: readers may find it helpful to know that when, for example, a recipe calls for folding egg whites, the glossary defines folding (page 280), and Useful Techniques explains exactly how to do it (page 275). Beginners in the kitchen should read through the section called Hints, Suggestions, and Shortcuts (page 263) before plunging in. The miscellaneous information and advice in that section are organized by subject, and the index contains references to all this material. The index also has listings for readers with special interests: "ethnic" recipes, meatless main dishes, diet recipes, leftovers and their uses, party foods, one-pot dinners, dinners that cook themselves, food for hot weather.

In addition to dispensing practical advice and facing the actual problems of the kitchen, this book attempts to introduce beginning cooks to a sampling of recipes from many different cultures—African, French, Italian, German, Greek, Oriental, and regional American. In the hope that new cooks will be adventurous, I have tried to introduce what may be unfamiliar vegetables or new ways of preparing familiar ones.

Perhaps the chief problem an inexperienced cook faces is how to get everything done at the same time—how to coordinate the cooking of three different dishes for the same meal, how to get it all together. Practice and staying calm will help, but so will some planning. Begin with whatever takes longest to cook, and when that is under way, start the dish that takes somewhat less time to cook. Some dishes can be fixed ahead of time, and doubling a recipe in order to have at least one dish already cooked for the next meal makes life that much easier. (See page 270 for suggestions for second-night food.) On the whole, vegetables take a short time to cook, so cook them last. Until you're experienced, try only one new dish at a meal, and rely on two recipes you've already tried. The long-cooking recipes, for example, Black Bean Soup, Corned Beef, or roasts and their accompaniments, are not "quick" meals, but they are quick to put up, and they do free you to do other things—or nothing at all—while they cook their allotted time.

A good many restaurants offer dishes that are not much more complicated than the dishes that novices in the kitchen can cook using this book. Simple rather than elaborate, such food depends on the freshness and quality of the ingredients and the care with which they are used. Even people who are busy and tired can give their full attention to cooking when there are so few ingredients and so few directions. I have used all these recipes; I have invented many of them. They have proved to me that good cooking doesn't have to be time-consuming or expensive—or unhealthy. These recipes are simple enough to be used every day yet good enough to be used for guests, but perhaps learning to cook well means cooking well for all occasions.

A BASIC
SEASONING SHELF

Herbs and spices are used to improve or enhance the flavor of food, to make it more interesting and delicious. Herbs come from the leaves of plants that grow in temperate climates, spices from the dried seeds and barks of tropical plants. *An alphabetical list of the herbs and spices you will need appears on pages 246–252.* Other commonly used seasoning agents include garlic, onion or scallion, lemons, limes, and oranges—all easy to keep on hand.

Fresh herbs

If you have an herb garden or have a friend with one, you are plainly at an advantage. But if you have only a windowsill, you can raise some of the hardier herbs—basil, chives, parsley, and rosemary—in pots. Even if you must depend solely on the supermarket, you can at least find fresh parsley, which is available all year around in most produce sections and is very inexpensive. Fresh parsley is incomparably better than the dried variety sold in jars. If you buy a fresh bunch every week and store it, washed and shaken dry, in your refrigerator in a jar with a screw-on lid or in a plastic bag with a moistened paper towel, the parsley will last for a week and you will have both a fine source of flavor and a pleasant garnish for a good many dishes.

Dried herbs

A good formula to follow if you must depend on dried herbs, and most of us must, is:

1 tablespoon chopped fresh = 1 teaspoon dried

In other words, a 3-to-1 ratio. Dried herbs are supposedly stronger than fresh, but if your jars of herbs have been sitting over the kitchen stove for a few years, whatever is in those jars will probably have deteriorated so much that it will do little for the flavor of your dish. If you can't use fresh herbs, at least use relatively fresh dried herbs, and beware of extraordinary pallor in green herbs: as with human beings, it may signify that all is not well.

It's best, then, to store herbs away from the heat and to buy them in smaller quantities than those sold in uniform jars in the supermarket, tempting as they may look. Instead, you may want to take the trouble to go to a specialty shop that sells herbs and spices in bulk. Buy *small* amounts so that they keep their true flavor, and store them in the little vials that come from the pharmacy: many pharmacists will sell them for token sums. Label them clearly and attractively, and you will have taken a great step forward.

Don't bother with boxes of ready-ground pepper. Instead, buy whole peppercorns and grind them in your pepper mill or, for particular dishes like steak *au poivre*, crush the peppercorns with a mortar and pestle. Nutmeg too should be bought whole rather than ground: it is simple to grate, and the flavor is far better.

Garlic

Fresh garlic can be found in the produce section of the supermarket. Keep a head of garlic in the refrigerator and never allow yourself to run out of it.

The recipes in this book call for a variety of ways of attacking the garlic bulb: mashing,* mincing, slicing, pressing, or cutting a clove to rub a salad bowl. It is all worth the effort. Use garlic powder only when you are in a tearing rush or a state of extraordinary fatigue, or when you are applying a great many herbs and spices, as, say, to the Baked Spiced Chicken recipe (page 79). But try to avoid garlic salt, which bears very little relation to real garlic and, more-

---

* The easiest way to mash a garlic clove is to place it on a cutting board after peeling, of course. Take a flat-bottomed drinking glass and push down. Make a few cuts in the garlic clove with a sharp vegetable knife.

over, may result in oversalting in recipes that call for an exact amount of salt. A last word on fresh garlic: take care not to burn it in sautéing (scorched garlic can ruin a dish). If you do burn it, discard the oil and garlic and begin again.

Onions

It would be hard to imagine a working kitchen without a few onions on hand. If the onion you reach for is strong rather than sweet (and you will know instantly), dice it as finely as possible to reduce its potency, particularly in uncooked dishes like salads. Because scallions need no peeling and cause no suffering, it's wise to pick up a fresh bunch every week at the supermarket. Scallions are, in most cases, an excellent substitute for onions and, unlike onions, an attractive garnish when finely minced.

Fresh ginger

Fresh ginger root can be found in the supermarket; store it in the freezer and grate it whenever you need it.

Lemons and oranges

Although lemons and oranges (and why not limes?) are neither herbs nor spices, they are wonderful flavoring agents and will last for weeks. With fresh parsley, real garlic, fresh ginger, onions, scallions, and lemon and orange juice and zest (the colored peel, without the white part), you will be at a perpetual advantage: these are powerful allies always within reach.

Condiments

Condiments like Dijon mustard, Worcestershire sauce, and soy sauce (see listing on page 253) are best kept on shelves inside the refrigerator door.

Salt

How much salt is a difficult subject. Beginning cooks need explicit directions, and as a good friend pointed out to me, for her the hardest part of learning to cook was learning to determine the correct amount of salt when recipes give merely "salt and pepper" as ingredients or "salt to taste" as a direction. On the other hand, tastes vary, and perhaps nowhere more than in the matter of salt. There is an astonishing range in judgments of what is salty enough and what is not, but even more important, we have been learning from the medical profession how harmful large amounts of salt can be for many people. For these reasons, I have fallen back on the cowardly and persistent "salt to taste" formula. When I do state amounts, I tend, on the whole, to salt timidly. The reader may work up to the amounts he or she wishes.

Two cardinal principles

1. *Never* pour directly from a spice bottle into anything you are preparing: measure, and if you are ever in doubt when you are inventing a dish, use less of the herb or spice rather than more, and add gradually, tasting all the while. The point is to heighten rather than overwhelm the effect of a dish.

2. *Always* correct the seasoning. That means, quite simply, taste what you have cooked before you serve it, and make any last-minute adjustments that may elevate the dish to new heights.

Note on the Recipes

When reference is made to recipes in the book, the recipe title is capitalized.

Unless otherwise specified:
   butter is unsalted butter
   cream is sweet cream
   flour is all-purpose flour
   sugar is granulated sugar
   brown sugar can be either light or dark, as you prefer
   pepper is freshly ground pepper.

APPETIZERS

Shrimp Spread

This filling, made with a food processor or blender, is excellent with crackers or in thin sandwiches.

½ lemon
4 ounces tiny fresh cooked shrimp, shelled and chilled, or 4½-ounce can tiny shrimp, chilled and drained
1 stick butter, at room temperature

1 teaspoon Worcestershire sauce
several sprigs fresh parsley

1 Squeeze the lemon.

2 In a food processor blend the shrimp, butter, lemon juice, Worcestershire sauce, and parsley.

3 Place in a bowl and chill before serving. Serve with triangles or squares of thinly sliced bread or with crackers.

Serves 6 to 8

Sardines in Cream

If you think you don't like sardines, you may be surprised at how good they can be, prepared this way. And remember, they are very rich in calcium.

3¾-ounce can sardines
(preferably water-
packed)
1 small tart apple
3 tablespoons light or
heavy cream

salt and pepper to taste

Optional:
½ stalk celery, finely
chopped

1 Drain the sardines, place them in a bowl, and mash them with a fork.

2 Peel and core the apple and chop it finely.

3 Add the apple (and celery if desired) to the sardines. Add the cream and mix well. Season with salt and pepper. Serve with crackers.

Serves 6

Marinated Scallops, or Ceviche

The lime juice marinade in this recipe does the "cooking," and you have nothing more to do than serve the scallops with crusty French or Italian bread as a first course. You can substitute any firm-fleshed fish for the scallops, if you wish: try bluefish, for example, or red snapper, or mackerel.

3 limes
½ Bermuda onion or 4 scallions
½ pound fresh scallops

¼ teaspoon chili powder
1 clove garlic, peeled and minced
small handful parsley, minced
salt and pepper to taste

Optional:
1 tomato and 1 peeled avocado, cut in chunks

1 Squeeze the limes.

2 Chop the onion or scallions finely. If the scallops are large, cut them in small pieces, no larger than quarters.

3 Mix the lime juice, onions or scallions, and the seasonings in a nonmetallic bowl and add the scallops, making sure they are completely covered with the marinade. Cover and chill at least 6 hours. Garnish, if you wish, with tomato and avocado before serving.

Serves 3 to 4

Caviar Spread

There are two kinds of caviar—the kind you can't afford and the kind you can. This is a good recipe for the latter.

8-ounce container sour cream
3-ounce package Philadelphia cream cheese
2-ounce jar black or red lumpfish caviar

Optional:
1 *lemon, sliced*

1 Blend the sour cream and cream cheese in a processor or blender.

2 Transfer the mixture to a wide bowl and cover. Refrigerate.

3 Just before serving, spread the caviar on the surface of the mixture. If you like, accompany the bowl with a small dish of halved lemon slices. Serve with thinly sliced pumpernickel.

Serves 8

Baba Ghanouj, or Eggplant Salad

This recipe uses tahini, a paste of sesame seeds common in Mediterranean cooking. Tahini can be found in Middle Eastern grocery stores, health food stores, and some supermarkets. Served with pita, baba ghanouj makes an excellent appetizer.

1 medium eggplant
juice of 1 lemon
¼ cup tahini

½ teaspoon salt
1 clove garlic, peeled
small handful fresh parsley
1 teaspoon sugar

Optional:
toasted sesame seeds

1 Bake the whole eggplant in a 350° or 400° oven for about 40 minutes, or until the eggplant seems to shrivel.

2 Cut away the stem and green hull from the top, and cut the eggplant into quarters.

3 Place the eggplant and all the other ingredients in the blender or the food processor and process just until all the ingredients are blended. Do not overprocess. Garnish, if you wish, with toasted sesame seeds.

Serves 4

Baked Mushrooms

These mushrooms are particularly good and offer a fairly easy way to provide finger food for a number of people.

2 slices bacon
½ pound medium-sized mushrooms
3-ounce package Philadelphia cream cheese

pepper to taste

Preheat the oven to 300°.

1 Fry the bacon, drain the strips on a paper towel, and crumble.

2 Wash and dry the mushrooms (or, as some cooks prefer, simply wipe them with a damp cloth). Remove the stems from the mushrooms and save them for another use, such as in an omelet.

3 Fill each mushroom cap with as much of the cream cheese as you neatly can. Top with crumbled bacon, pressing it lightly into the cheese. Bake 10 to 15 minutes, or until lightly browned on top. Do not let the bacon burn. Season with pepper.

Serves 3 to 4

Hard-Cooked Eggs with Mayonnaise

This is a standard first course in France. If you hard-cook the eggs properly (see the instructions on page 276), make your own mayonnaise, and present the dish attractively, you will have a first-rate appetizer.

2 hard-cooked eggs
½ cup mayonnaise preferably homemade (page 174)
½ teaspoon capers

sprinkling of:
dried chervil
or
dried tarragon
or
fresh chives
or
finely minced fresh parsley

1 Peel the eggs and carefully cut them in half lengthwise.

2 Place the egg halves flat side down on individual plates. Add enough mayonnaise to cover each egg completely.

3 Garnish with capers and the herb you choose.

Serves 2

Broiled Grapefruit

This may be baked rather than broiled: either way, it's a good candidate for brunch.

1 grapefruit
2 tablespoons maple syrup or light brown sugar
2 teaspoons bourbon

Preheat the broiler.

1 Cut the grapefruit in half and free the pulp as best you can so that it can be easily removed with a spoon.

2 Pour the maple syrup and bourbon over each half.

3 Broil until thoroughly heated.

Serves 2

FOUR-INGREDIENT RECIPES

Open Shrimp Sandwiches

Perfect with drinks, these sandwiches also make an elegant lunch, preceded by soup and followed by a substantial dessert.

1 cucumber, peeled
4 ounces tiny fresh cooked shrimp, shelled and chilled, or 4½-ounce can tiny shrimp, chilled and drained
¼ cup sour cream
Buttered thinly sliced pumpernickel

¼ teaspoon dried dillweed
salt and pepper to taste

Optional:
lemon juice

1 Cut the cucumber into very thin slices. Salt, chill for an hour or more, and drain.

2 Mix the shrimp with sour cream; add dillweed, salt, and pepper.

3 Immediately before serving, spread the shrimp mixture on buttered pumpernickel. Place 2 or 3 cucumber slices on each open sandwich and serve with freshly ground pepper and a few drops of lemon juice, if you wish.

Serves 4 to 6

Chopped Chicken Livers

There are purists and there are impurists in respect to this dish. The controversial point seems to be chicken fat vs. butter. On neutral ground, I offer either one.

1 medium onion
2 tablespoons chicken fat
  or butter
½ pound chicken livers
2 hard-cooked eggs,
  shelled

salt and pepper to taste

1 Peel and slice the onion. Melt the chicken fat or butter in a skillet over medium-high heat; add the onion and sauté briefly until it is translucent (7 to 10 minutes).

2 Push the onion to the sides of the skillet; add the livers and sauté them 2 to 5 minutes until they are brown on the outside.

3 Place the onion, livers, and eggs in a processor or blender and process briefly until all the ingredients are blended together. Season and serve with sesame crackers.

Serves 6

Other Suggestions for Appetizers

For other first-course possibilities, see the following recipes. (Since these are main-dish recipes, you may wish to serve smaller portions than are called for.)

Scallops in the Shell (page 97)
Broiled Shrimp, or Scampi (page 98)
Simple Salmon Timbale (page 105)
Eggs with Ham or Asparagus in
  Cheese Sauce (page 110)
Ricotta Pie (page 111)
Fried Cheese, or Saganaki (page 112)
Cheese Timbale (page 118)
Steamed Vegetables (page 121) with
  Green Sauce (page 178)
Fresh Beets with Dill (page 123)
Marinated Leeks (page 133)
Roasted Peppers (page 136)
Apple and Beet Salad (page 155)
White Bean Salad (page 156)
Cucumber Salad (page 158)
Egg Salad (page 160)
Ham and Melon Salad (page 162)
Smoked Fish Salad (page 169)
Cheese Straws (page 239)
Eggs Kiev (page 240)

Note: If you wish to serve a fish course as part of a more elaborate dinner, any of the recipes in Chapter 5 will do.

SOUPS

Curried Spinach Soup

A dependable soup hot or chilled. If you wish to serve it chilled, first allow it to cool to room temperature before placing it in the refrigerator. (If you prefer to use fresh spinach, allow 1 pound and cook covered 2 to 3 minutes.)

10-ounce package frozen chopped spinach
2 cups beef or chicken stock, or 2 bouillon cubes in 2 cups water
3-ounce package Philadelphia cream cheese

1 teaspoon curry powder
3 tablespoons chopped fresh chives or 1 scallion, chopped
small bunch fresh parsley
½ teaspoon powdered cumin
salt and pepper to taste

1 Cook the spinach and the curry powder in the stock, covered, about 6 minutes from the time the water comes to the boil, or just until the spinach is defrosted. Be sure not to add salt at this time or to let the spinach lose its color.

2 Empty the contents of the pot into the blender. Add the cream cheese, chives, parsley, and cumin. Blend thoroughly, holding down the lid of the blender jar firmly. Add salt and pepper.

3 Reheat just before serving, but do not allow the soup to boil or the delicate flavor will be spoiled.

Note: In making this and other blender soups, see the tip in the Hints, Suggestions, and Shortcuts section (page 263).

Serves 4

Cabbage Soup or Onion Soup*

The method used here is also the basic method for French Onion Soup (see below).

3 tablespoons butter or safflower or corn oil
½ small head green cabbage, thinly sliced
4 cups beef or chicken stock, or 4 bouillon cubes and 4 cups water

1 clove garlic, peeled and minced
1 teaspoon dried dillweed
½ teaspoon dried thyme
salt and pepper to taste

Optional:
2 tablespoons sour cream or yogurt

1 Using a 2-quart saucepan, heat the butter or oil with the seasonings.

2 Add the cabbage to the sizzling, aromatized oil and sauté over medium-high heat, stirring often, until the volume reduces and the cabbage begins to brown. This will occur in a few minutes.

3 Add the stock and bring to a boil. Lower the heat and cover, stirring from time to time. Cook 10 minutes. Garnish, if you wish, with sour cream or yogurt.

Serves 4

* For French Onion Soup, simply use 4 large onions, sliced thinly, instead of the cabbage, and omit the dill and thyme. Sauté onions, covered, over low heat for 20 to 30 minutes; a large pinch of sugar added to the sautéing onions will help them brown. Onion soup should be garnished with toast covered with grated Swiss or Parmesan cheese, then toasted or broiled.

Chilled Beet Soup, or Borscht

You may wish to vary this traditional recipe with 1 cup beef stock or ½ teaspoon dried dillweed. See page 123 for directions on cooking beets.

3–4 cooked beets, peeled and sliced

2 cups cooking liquid from beets

2 tablespoons plus 2 teaspoons sour cream

salt and pepper to taste

Optional:
juice of ½ lemon

1 Blend the beets, liquid, and 2 tablespoons of sour cream together. Add seasoning to taste.

2 Chill for 3 to 4 hours.

3 Pour into bowls and stir in a few drops of lemon juice, if you wish. Garnish each bowl with a heaping teaspoon of sour cream.

Serves 2

Cold Cucumber Soup

This is a no-cook, no-frills method that produces immediate and very acceptable results.

2 cucumbers
2 scallions
1 cup sour cream or yogurt

¼ teaspoon powdered cumin
¼ teaspoon garlic powder
salt and pepper to taste

1 Peel the cucumbers and cut into 2-inch segments. Wash and trim the scallions and cut them into 2-inch lengths.

2 Place all the ingredients and seasonings in the blender jar and blend thoroughly.

3 Chill the soup thoroughly (3 to 4 hours) before serving.

Serves 2

Dieter's Mushroom Soup

This recipe is suitable for a low-cholesterol as well as a low-calorie diet. Dieters sustaining themselves on this soup will have no reason for self-pity: they will be eating very well.

½ pound mushrooms
1 cup chicken stock, or 1
    bouillon cube and 1 cup
    water
1 cup low-fat or skim milk

¼ teaspoon freshly grated
    nutmeg
salt and pepper to taste

Optional:
1 tablespoon dry sherry

1 Clean and slice the mushrooms (see page 148).

2 Place them in a saucepan with the broth, bring to a boil, and simmer 10 minutes.

3 Place the mushrooms, broth, and milk in the blender container. Add the seasonings and blend for 20 seconds. Add the sherry, if you wish.

Serves 2

Emergency Tomato Soup

If you're dieting, substitute yogurt for the sour cream; garnish the soup with chopped chives or scallions, minced parsley, or sliced water chestnuts.

1½ cups tomato or V-8
  juice
1 cup chicken or beef stock,
  or 1 bouillon cube and 1
  cup water
2 heaping tablespoons plus
  2 teaspoons sour cream

½ teaspoon dried basil
salt and pepper to taste

Optional:
2-inch strip orange peel

1 Blend juice, stock, 2 tablespoons sour cream, orange peel (if you wish), and seasonings.

2 Pour into a saucepan and heat carefully on low heat, being sure to keep the soup from boiling. Correct the seasoning.

3 Serve and garnish with a heaping teaspoon of sour cream for each bowl.

Note: For cold soup, omit Step 2 and chill for 3 to 4 hours before serving.

Serves 2

FOUR-INGREDIENT RECIPES

Potato and Onion Soup

This soup is simple, sustaining, and equally good hot or chilled. Served chilled, it is a variant of vichyssoise.*

2 medium onions
3 medium potatoes
2 tablespoons butter
3 cups chicken or beef
   stock, or 3 bouillon cubes
   and 3 cups water

¼ teaspoon dried thyme
salt and pepper to taste

Optional:
heavy or sour cream
¼ teaspoon minced fresh
   chives

1 Peel and dice the onions and potatoes.

2 In a pot, melt the butter and sauté the vegetables on low heat for about 10 minutes, covered. Add the seasonings.

3 Add the chicken or beef stock and bring to a boil. Lower the heat, cover the pot, and cook for 15 minutes. Garnish with 1 tablespoon of heavy cream or sour cream and chives, if you wish.

Serves 4

* As vichyssoise, the soup should be smoothly blended and then chilled for 3 to 4 hours.

Egg and Lemon Soup,
or Avgolemono

Homemade stock is essential for this classic Greek soup. You
will need a hand-held beater for this recipe (or a wire whisk)
and an untiring arm.

4 cups homemade chicken
   stock (page 276)
¼ cup long-grain rice
1 large lemon or 2 small
   ones
2 eggs

salt and pepper to taste

1 Bring the broth to a boil in a deep pot and add the rice.
Simmer for 20 minutes. Remove from the heat.

2 Squeeze the lemons. In a large bowl, beat the eggs and
add the lemon juice, beating again. In a steady stream, slowly
add a ladleful of soup, beating steadily.

3 Pour the mixture back to the remaining soup, beating
all the while. Once combined, the soup should not be allowed
to boil. Correct the seasoning. Serve at once.

Serves 4

Cock-a-Leekie Soup

Other sliced vegetables—a carrot, a stalk of celery, a small onion—any or all can be added to this very satisfying soup in Step 2.

2 cups chicken stock
¼ cup quick-cooking
  barley*
1 leek
½ cup light cream or milk

salt and pepper to taste

1 Bring the chicken stock to a boil. Add the barley, lower the heat, cover, and cook on low heat for 25 minutes.

2 Wash the leek (see page 132) and slice it. Add it to the soup, together with the seasonings. Bring to a boil, lower the heat, cover, and cook another 15 minutes.

3 Add the cream or milk. Heat, but do not allow the soup to boil.

Serves 2

  *Be sure to use quick-cooking barley, as regular barley takes much longer to cook.

Black Bean Soup

This very good soup requires a little preliminary homework. The night before, pick over the beans, remove any pebbles, and wash. Cover the beans with water and let them soak overnight.

1 cup dried black beans, soaked overnight

2 onions, peeled, or 1 tablespoon preserved onions*

¼-pound sliced ham, diced or leftover ham bone

1 jigger dry sherry

1 clove garlic, peeled
½ teaspoon celery seed
2 bay leaves
salt and pepper to taste

Optional:
2 carrots, sliced, to be added the last half hour of cooking

1 Drain the beans. Boil 6 cups of water and add the beans, together with all the remaining ingredients except the sherry.

2 Bring back to a boil and lower the heat. Cover and simmer the beans 3 to 4 hours, or until they are tender.

3 Before serving, remove the bay leaf and the ham bone, if it is used. Add the sherry. Stir, taste, and correct the seasoning. The soup can be garnished with sour cream, minced raw onion, chopped hard-cooked egg, or chopped tangerine sections!

Serves 4

* Preserved onions, a good substitute for fresh onions in soups or stews, are sold in crocks in Oriental shops.

Blender Plum Soup

Fruit soups are not as widely appreciated in the United States as they are in Europe, though they ought to be: they are very refreshing in the summer and easily made.

1 small lemon
28-ounce can whole purple plums, pitted (including juice)
⅓ cup red wine
¼ cup sugar

⅛ teaspoon ground cinnamon
⅛ teaspoon powdered cloves

Optional:
sour cream

1 Squeeze the lemon and pour the juice into the blender container.

2 Add all the other ingredients and blend well.

3 If you like a sweeter soup, add more sugar cautiously. Chill. Garnish each bowl, if you wish, with a tablespoon of sour cream.

Serves 4

Avocado Soup

One of the best of all the quick summer soups.

1 avocado	½ teaspoon picante sauce
1 lime	small handful fresh parsley
1 cup milk	salt to taste
1 scallion	

1 Peel the avocado and remove the pit.

2 Squeeze the lime and remove any seeds from the juice.

3 Place all the ingredients in the blender and blend until the mixture is perfectly smooth. Correct the seasoning. Refrigerate for 3 to 4 hours and serve well chilled.

Serves 2

Tomato-Potato Soup

This is a favorite hot winter soup of a family of soup-lovers; this recipe is perfect with a soufflé-bread-salad meal and fine as a first course at dinner parties.

2 large onions
4 tablespoons butter
4 medium potatoes
46-ounce can tomato or
   V-8 juice

½ teaspoon celery seed
salt and pepper to taste

Optional:
1–2 teaspoons light brown
    sugar

1 Peel and dice the onions. Meanwhile, melt the butter over low heat. Raise the heat to medium-high, add the onions, and sauté until they are lightly brown (10 to 20 minutes).

2 Add 2 cups of water, mix well, and simmer for 30 minutes.

3 Meanwhile, peel and dice the potatoes. Add the potatoes and tomato or V-8 juice to the onion mixture and bring to a boil. Lower the heat and boil gently until the potatoes are just tender, about 8 to 10 minutes. If you need more liquid, add more tomato juice. Add the celery seed, salt, and pepper, and, if you like, the brown sugar.

Serves 6

MEAT

Saltimbocca

The name of this Italian dish literally means "jump-in-the-mouth." It is as simple to prepare as it is deserving of its name. Serve with Braised Celery or Grated Sauteed Zucchini.

½–¾ pound veal, cut for
  scallopine
6 small slices prosciutto or
  thinly cut cooked ham
2 tablespoons butter

pepper to taste
½ teaspoon dried sage

Optional:
6 thin slices Fontina or
  Swiss cheese

1 Sprinkle each slice of veal with pepper and sage. Cut each slice of prosciutto to cover a slice of veal. If you wish, cut the cheese in the same way and place a slice between the veal and the prosciutto.

2 Melt the butter in a skillet, add the meat and cook over high heat for only a few minutes on each side.

3 Transfer to a small heated platter. Deglaze the pan* with a tablespoon or two of water, and pour the juices over the meat.

Serves 2 generously

* See page 280 for instructions on deglazing.

Veal Parmesan

You may substitute thinly sliced breast of chicken or turkey for the scallopine. Serve with Roasted or Simmered Peppers.

4 tablespoons freshly grated Parmesan cheese

½–¾ pound veal, cut for scallopine

3 tablespoons butter or olive oil

salt and pepper to taste

Optional:
watercress or parsley

1 Distribute the Parmesan cheese evenly on a large plate. Season with salt and pepper.

2 Dip the pieces of veal in the cheese, coating both sides.

3 Heat the butter or oil in a skillet over medium-high heat. When it is sizzling, add the veal and sauté rapidly, allowing no more than 3 minutes on each side, turning once. Garnish with watercress or parsley, if desired.

Note: If you substitute chicken or turkey, you will need to sauté the pieces a minute longer on each side.

Serves 2 generously

Lamb Korma

This is a wonderfully fragrant curry, and exceptionally easy to prepare. A *korma* is a curry with a yogurt-based sauce. This one will accommodate the toughest cuts of lamb. For best results, cut away as much of the fat as possible. Serve with rice or bulgur wheat.

2 pounds stewing lamb, cut into cubes
2 medium onions, sliced
2 cups yogurt or sour cream (or a combination)

2 sticks cinnamon
1 teaspoon ground cloves
10 peppercorns
2 teaspoons ground cardamom
2 teaspoons ground coriander
1 teaspoon to 1 tablespoon chili powder
salt to taste

1 Place all the ingredients in a heavy pan with a tight-fitting lid and pour in enough water to nearly cover the mixture.

2 Cover and cook over low heat 2 hours, or until the meat is done, removing the lid once or twice to stir the *korma*.

3 When the meat is done, remove it from the pot. Discard the cinnamon sticks and the peppercorns and boil down the sauce until it thickens, about 10 minutes. Briefly return the meat to the pot to warm it.

Serves 4 generously

Lamb Shanks

The long cooking develops the flavor of the shanks and makes them very tender. Serve with new potatoes, rice, bulgur wheat, or barley.

2 pounds lamb shanks
2 onions
6-ounce can tomato paste
plus ½ cup water

1 clove garlic, peeled and minced
½ teaspoon dried thyme
½ teaspoon dried oregano
1 bay leaf
salt and pepper to taste

1 Using a bit of lamb fat, grease the bottom of a saucepan. Add the shanks and brown over medium heat.

2 Peel and slice the onions, and when the shanks have browned, push them to the side and sauté the onions.

3 Add the tomato paste, water, and seasonings and simmer covered 2½ hours, stirring from time to time and adding a little water as necessary. Remove the bay leaf before serving.

Serves 2

Baked Ham

Baking this quantity of ham for two people means you'll have something to fall back on for succeeding meals. Ham keeps better than other roasts, losing none of its flavor or texture as you take slices from it in the course of a week. Serve with baked potatoes and a green salad.

3-pound cooked boneless
  ham
¾ cup orange juice
¼ cup orange marmalade
  (preferably the bitter
  or Seville variety)

¼ teaspoon mustard
  powder
whole cloves

Preheat the oven to 350°.

1 Score the ham* and press a clove into the center of each diamond.

2 Place the ham on a rack in a baking pan and bake uncovered for 30 minutes.

3 Mix the orange juice with the marmalade. Pour the mixture over the ham and bake for 30 minutes, basting every 10 minutes. (The meat thermometer should register 140° when it is done.) Remove the ham to a platter to carve.

Note: If all the liquid is absorbed, add a little water to the bottom of the pan. In any case, don't allow the glaze on the bottom of the pan to burn.

Serves 8

   * See page 281 for instructions on scoring.

Ham in Madeira or Red Wine

Serve this delicious ham with spinach.

1 tablespoon butter or safflower or corn oil
2 thick slices cooked ham (about ½ pound)
½ cup Madeira or red wine

1 clove garlic, peeled and minced
handful parsley, minced

1 Heat the butter or oil in a skillet over medium-high heat and sauté the slices of ham in the butter or oil.

2 Add the garlic and wine.

3 Cook uncovered for 15 minutes, turning the ham a few times. Add the parsley during the last few minutes of cooking.

Serves 2

Ham Stew

This recipe can be greatly enlarged and made even more interesting if you wish (see below); either way—in its most basic form, or with additions, it is an unusual stew, and one that solves the problem of what to do with leftover ham.

2 ham slices (about ½ pound), cut into cubes
1 medium onion
¾ cup apple cider or juice

¼ teaspoon ground cloves
¼ teaspoon ground cinnamon
salt and pepper to taste

1 Trim off the fat and use a piece of the fat to grease the bottom of a saucepan. Peel and slice the onion.

2 Heat the pan, and when the fat is hot, add the sliced onion. Sauté until golden, then add the ham, mixing the onion and ham for 3 to 4 minutes over medium heat.

3 Add the apple cider and seasonings. Simmer gently 10 minutes, covered.

Note: To make a more varied stew, add any or all of the following:
4 potatoes, peeled (or unpeeled but scrubbed) and sliced
2 apples, unpeeled, cored, and sliced
½ small cabbage, cut in eighths
6 fresh Italian prune plums, pitted, or dried prunes, pitted
2 carrots, pared or scrubbed and sliced
small handful raisins or currants
Cover and simmer together 25 to 30 minutes after bringing to a boil. You may need to add a little more liquid.

Serves 2

Pork Chops and Wine

This basic top-of-the-stove recipe can also be used for lamb or veal chops. Simply shorten the cooking time in Step 3 to 15 minutes for well-done lamb and veal. Serve with Brussels Sprouts with Fennel or Steamed Cucumbers and Blue Cheese.

2 large or 4 small pork chops	¼ teaspoon each dried thyme, marjoram, and basil
1 tablespoon flour	salt and pepper to taste
¼ cup red wine	

1 Trim the fat from the chops. Heat a heavy frying pan; add a bit of the trimmed fat and push it around the pan with a fork until all the surface is well greased.

2 Dust the chops with flour, salt, and pepper, and sprinkle them with ⅛ teaspoon of each of the herbs. Brown the chops over medium-high heat and turn, sprinkling with the rest of the herbs.

3 When browned, add the wine, lower the heat, cover, and cook for 25 minutes.

Serves 2

Sweet and Sour Pork Chops

For best results, use the Cranberry Relish on page 192 to prepare this dish. Serve with French-Fried Sweet Potatoes and a green salad.

2 large or 4 small pork chops
4 tablespoons cranberry relish
1 tablespoon cider vinegar

salt and pepper to taste

Optional:
sprinkling of brown sugar

1 Trim the chops, removing as much of the fat as you can, and season them. Rub the pan with some of the fat.

2 Over medium-high heat, brown the chops well on each side. Reduce the heat, cover the pan, and cook the chops gently for 20 minutes.

3 Uncover the pan and add the cranberry relish and vinegar. If you wish, add the brown sugar. Cook 8 to 10 minutes longer, turning the chops in the sauce a few times. Correct the seasoning.

Serves 2

Spare Ribs

This recipe uses a combination of baking and broiling to reduce the risk of burned ribs. Serve with French-Fried Sweet Potatoes or Appalachian Corn Bread.

1¼ cups Sweet and Sour Barbecue Sauce (page 189)
½ cup any fruit juice
4 pounds spare ribs

1 Add the fruit juice to the barbecue sauce and stir well. Cover the ribs with the mixture.

2 Refrigerate 4 to 6 hours, turning from time to time.

3 Transfer the ribs and marinade to a heatproof dish and bake in a 325° oven for an hour and 10 minutes, turning the ribs once or twice, and basting when necessary; finish by browning them in the broiler or over charcoal for another 20 minutes. The ribs should be a rich brown on both sides.

Serves 4

Middle Eastern Hamburgers

If you sauté the onion *before* mixing with the meat, the flavor will be better. If you mix the meat with all the seasonings an hour or so before cooking, the flavor will be still better. Serve with Mashed Potatoes.

2 tablespoons safflower or corn oil
¾ pound ground beef, or lamb if you prefer
1 medium onion

½ teaspoon dried mint
½ teaspoon dried oregano
¼ teaspoon ground cloves
¼ teaspoon ground cinnamon
¼ teaspoon garlic powder
salt and pepper to taste

1 Heat the oil in a skillet over medium-high heat. Chop the onion finely. Sauté the onion and allow it to cool.

2 Mix the onion and the seasonings with the meat. Shape into 4 patties.

3 Sauté the patties in the same pan over medium heat, about 3 to 4 minutes on each side for medium rare, or a little longer for well done.

Serves 2 generously

Chili Con Carne

This recipe is not much harder than opening a can of chili, but it's so much better. It requires opening *two* cans and browning the meat, but that's really all. And there's still only one pot to wash. Double the recipe for a second meal: the flavor ripens and the chili is all the better the next night. This recipe makes a medium-hot chili; use less chili powder if you like. Serve with Appalachian Corn Bread.

½ pound hamburger meat
16-ounce can red beans*
14½-ounce can whole
    tomatoes

2 tablespoons chili powder
1 tablespoon powdered
  cumin

Optional:
1 medium onion, chopped

1 Place the meat (and the onion if you wish) in a heavy pan and cook over medium-high heat, stirring constantly to avoid sticking (there should be no need to add fat; no doubt there's enough in the ground meat).

2 When the meat browns, add the beans and tomatoes with their juice, together with the chili powder and cumin. Mix well, mashing the tomatoes.

3 Lower the heat and simmer uncovered for 30 minutes. Add salt and pepper.

Note: Since chili powders vary in their degree of hotness, you may want to halve the chili powder called for, adding more to taste, as you wish. For a hotter chili, add 1 teaspoon cayenne pepper or 1 teaspoon crushed red chili peppers.

Serves 2

* You may wish to drain the beans and rinse them under cold water to reduce the amount of starch and sugar.

Shish Kebab

"Shish kebab" (literal translation—"skewered meat") are pieces of tender beef, lamb, pork, veal, or chicken that have been marinated for a few hours, then threaded on a skewer and grilled over a charcoal fire or under a hot broiler on a rack. The marinade seasons or aromatizes the meat, makes it tender, and glazes the surface. Baste the meat as soon as it begins to look dry and keep watching and basting. It's best not to pierce it with a fork: you don't want to break the surface and risk losing the juice. Serve with rice.

Ingredients for threading

½ pound lean, tender meat, cut into 1-inch cubes
1 large onion, quartered, with the layers separated
2 tomatoes, quartered (or cherry tomatoes)

Optional:
bay leaves
mushroom caps, washed and dried
green and/or red peppers, cut into squares
water chestnuts
unpeeled eggplant, cut into small cubes

Basic method: See page 186 for a variety of marinades suitable for shish kebab.

1 Mix the ingredients for marinating in a bowl. Cut the meat into 1-inch cubes, place in a nonmetallic bowl, and cover with the marinade. Refrigerate overnight.

2 Thread the meat onto skewers, alternating with bits of bay leaf, if you wish, and any or all of the vegetables listed.

3 Grill over charcoal outdoors or under a preheated broiler in your kitchen. Turn often, until the desired degree of doneness is reached.
Serves 2 to 3

Chinese Stir-Fried Beef and Vegetables

This recipe illustrates the basic method of stir-frying (quick cooking in an uncovered wok or a skillet on high heat), which has become very popular in recent years and which is a very good thing to know about. It is a simple and satisfying way to produce a meal for one person or for many. You may substitute chicken or pork or bean curd (tofu)—although if you cook pork, you must be sure it is cooked thoroughly (5 minutes for thinly sliced pork over high heat); or you may vary the vegetables and change the proportions of vegetables to meat.

Stir-fried dishes can be very flexible, and there is little harm you can do the dish as long as you don't overcook the vegetables (or burn them). They should be as crisp as possible and the green vegetables should retain their bright color. Serve with rice. (For meatless dinners, that is, an all-vegetable stir-fry, serve brown rice or any other grain high in protein.)

1–2 cups vegetables—any one or a combination of: onion, celery, green pepper, cabbage, celery cabbage, bok choy, mushrooms, snow peas, water chestnuts, zucchini, spinach, bean sprouts

½ pound thinly sliced beef —good round or flank steak

2 tablespoons peanut, sesame, safflower, or corn oil*

1 teaspoon freshly grated ginger or ¼ teaspoon powdered ginger

1 clove garlic, peeled and minced

salt and pepper to taste

Optional:
unsalted peanuts, cashew nuts, almonds, or chopped scallions

* If you wish, you can double the amount of oil to 4 tablespoons; the more hot oil you use, the more thoroughly seared the meat will be.

1 Wash and chop the vegetables. Slice the beef (see page 265 for help in slicing meat thinly).

2 Heat the oil until sizzling and sauté the beef on medium-high heat (about 3 minutes), stirring occasionally. Add the seasonings and stir to mix with the beef.

3 Add the vegetables and continue to sauté and stir for about 4 minutes. Taste to make sure they are done.

Note: Traditionally, stir-frying is completed with the addition of Oriental Sauce (see recipe page 191). It is added at the last minute of cooking and is mixed through the ingredients. Allow 3 tablespoons for every ½ pound of meat or vegetables.

Serves 2 generously

Pepper Steak, or Steak *au Poivre*

This recipe may be adapted to ground beef of good quality (allow ½ pound for 2 servings)—in which case you have hamburger *au poivre*. Serve with baked potatoes.

1 pound Porterhouse or
  sirloin steak
2 tablespoons olive oil
2 tablespoons cognac

1 teaspoon cracked pepper-
  corns*
salt to taste

Optional:
2 teaspoons chopped fresh
  parsley
knob of butter or Herb
  Butter (page 190)

1 Trim off as much fat as possible. Cover one side of the steak with cracked pepper, pushing it into the meat so that it adheres. Turn the steak over and repeat the peppering on the other side.

2 Heat the oil in a cast-iron pan until it is very hot and add the steak. Cook a few minutes on each side over medium-high heat for rare steak; 4 minutes to a side for medium. Remove from the pan and place on a heated platter.

3 Deglaze the pan (see page 280) by placing over low heat and adding the cognac; scrape up particles of meat and juice and stir well for 2 or 3 minutes. Pour the cognac sauce over the steak and add salt to taste. Garnish, if you wish, with chopped parsley and/or a knob of butter or herb butter.

Serves 2

* Use either a mortar and pestle or a pepper mill.

FOUR-INGREDIENT RECIPES

Veal with Marsala

Since properly cut, first-rate scallopine is expensive and hard to find, thinly cut veal chops can be used in this recipe. Serve with Baked Fennel.

2 tablespoons flour
½–¾ pound boneless veal (or 1 pound veal chops or cutlets)
2 tablespoons butter
¼ cup Marsala wine or dry sherry

salt and pepper to taste

Optional:
thin lemon slices

1 Mix the flour with salt and pepper. Dip the veal in the seasoned flour.

2 Melt the butter over medium-high heat until the foam subsides, but do not let the butter burn. When it is hot and sizzling, add the veal, turning it once when it becomes golden brown.

3 Add the wine; lower the heat, turn the meat again, and cook gently for 2 to 3 minutes (allow 7 minutes a side for chops or cutlets). When the meat is done, remove it to a platter and scrape the pan, pouring the juices over the meat. Garnish with thinly cut slices of lemon, if desired.

Note: To test for doneness, cut with a sharp knife. The juices should not be red.

Serves 2 generously

Veal Piccata

For a more piquant flavor than usual, sauté a few teaspoons of capers in the butter along with the veal. Serve with broccoli.

½–¾ pound veal scallopine

2 small lemons

3 tablespoons butter

3 tablespoons dry white wine

salt and pepper to taste

Optional:
parsley sprigs

1 Cut the scallopine into small pieces. Squeeze the juice of 1½ lemons.

2 Put a skillet over medium-high heat and melt the butter. As soon as it sizzles, add the pieces of veal, allowing them to brown—2 to 3 minutes on each side.

3 Lower the heat and add the wine, scraping the pan and spooning the wine and meat sauce over the veal. With a slotted spoon, remove the veal to a heated platter and bring the sauce to a boil, stirring well. Pour over the veal and sprinkle with lemon juice. Garnish with slices from the remaining ½ lemon and a few sprigs of parsley if desired.

Serves 2 generously

Lamb Chops, Italian Style

You may want to add thinly sliced potatoes and zucchini—or either—to the lamb before adding the vermouth. If you add both, you'll have a complete meal in one pan.

1 onion
2 tablespoons olive oil
2 shoulder lamb chops
  trimmed of all fat
3 tablespoons dry ver-
  mouth or dry white wine

2 cloves garlic, peeled and
  chopped
pinch of dried rosemary
salt and pepper to taste

1 Peel and slice the onion. Heat the oil and, over medium heat, sauté the onion and chopped garlic until the onion is translucent.

2 Transfer the onion to a dish and over medium-high heat brown the lamb chops 2 to 3 minutes on each side. Cover with the sautéed onions.

3 Add the vermouth and seasonings and cover. Cook gently over low heat for 15 minutes.

Serves 2

Lamb or Beef with Bulgur Wheat

This is a four-ingredient version of *kibbee*, a Middle Eastern mixture that is generally served as little fried ovals. This version is moister and omits the final steps of shaping the mixture and frying. A green salad makes a good accompaniment. Consider this recipe when hungry teenagers burst through the door with their friends.

3 tablespoons olive, saf-
  flower, or corn oil,
  divided
½ cup medium bulgur
  wheat*
1 medium onion
½ pound lean ground
  lamb or ground round
  steak or chuck

*1 teaspoon dried mint or
  4 teaspoons fresh mint*
½ teaspoon ground cloves
*1–2 teaspoons ground
  cinnamon*
*½ teaspoon ground
  coriander*
*½–1 teaspoon powdered
  cumin*
several slivers orange peel
salt and pepper to taste

Optional:
*1 tablespoon pine nuts**

1 Heat 1½ cups of water to the boiling point. Cover and turn off the heat. Over medium-high heat, heat 2 tablespoons of oil in a large skillet. When the oil is sizzling, add the bulgur and stir. Reduce the heat to medium and continue to stir steadily until well coated with oil. Be careful not to burn it.

* Bulgur wheat is available in any Middle Eastern grocery or health food store. Pine nuts can be found in Middle Eastern or Italian groceries.

2 Place the bulgur in a bowl. Chop the onion. Add the third tablespoon of oil to the frying pan. When it is hot, sauté the meat with the onion and the seasonings. Put the bulgur back in the pan and mix well with the meat and onion.

3 Add the hot water and cover, cooking on low heat for 10 minutes. Stir a few times and correct the seasoning. When all the water is absorbed, transfer to a deep bowl. Garnish, if you wish, with pine nuts.

Serves 2

Beef and Spinach

This Italian stir-fry provides a lovely combination of flavors.
Serve it with rice or pasta.

10-ounce package frozen chopped spinach	*1 clove garlic, peeled and chopped*
½ pound lean round steak or flank steak	*⅛ teaspoon freshly grated nutmeg*
2 tablespoons olive oil	*salt and pepper to taste*
2 heaping teaspoons grated Parmesan cheese	

1 Cook the frozen spinach according to the directions.
Press out as much water as you can when you pour the
cooked spinach through a colander. (Better still, cook the
frozen spinach by placing it in a vegetable steamer standing
in ½ inch of water, and cover the pot. Bring to a boil and
then lower the heat. Cook until the spinach thaws.)

2 Meanwhile, trim the steak of as much fat as you can and
cut across the grain into thin slices. (See page 265 for directions on slicing meat.) Heat the oil, briefly sauté the garlic,
then add the meat and pan-fry it quickly over medium-high
heat.

3 Add the drained spinach and the cheese. Season with
nutmeg, salt, and pepper; mix well, and heat through.

Note: One-half pound of ground beef can be substituted for
the steak.

Serves 2

Beef and Brown Rice

This recipe is far more successful with brown rice than with white. It makes a satisfying and very good dinner, and one that children seem to like very much. Serve with "Crispy and Delicious" Green Beans.

1 teaspoon corn oil
2 medium onions or 6
   scallions, chopped
¾ pound ground beef
2 cups cooked brown rice*

1 clove garlic, peeled
   and minced
salt and pepper to taste

1 Heat the oil in a skillet. Peel and chop the onions (if you use scallions, wash them and pat them dry before cutting). Sauté the onions over medium-high heat for 7 to 10 minutes until golden.

2 Add the meat and sauté, stirring now and then to keep both onions and meat from burning. Add the garlic, salt, and pepper. Reduce the heat and cover.

3 Combine the brown rice with the contents of the skillet— preferably in an attractive bowl, and mix together.

Note: If you are using leftover cooked rice from the refrigerator, add it to the meat, stir well, and cover while you heat the mixture over low heat for a few minutes until it is hot.

Serves 2 generously

* See the directions on the package. Cooking time for brown rice varies from 20 to 45 minutes; it's important to know exactly how long the brand you use takes.

Beef Stew 1

This is a simple version of the traditional Belgian *carbonnades à la flamande* and goes well with Boiled New Potatoes or Mashed Potatoes.

2 onions
2 tablespoons safflower
    or corn oil
¾ pound stewing beef,
    cubed
½ can dark beer

1 *bay leaf*
1 *garlic clove, peeled and
    chopped*
¼ *teaspoon dried thyme*
1 *teaspoon sugar*
salt and pepper to taste

Optional:
1 *tablespoon flour*

1 Peel and slice the onions. Heat the oil and gently sauté the onions and garlic, 8 to 10 minutes. If you wish, throw a tablespoon of flour over the onions after they have become soft, to help thicken the stew.

2 Add the beef, the beer, and the seasonings.

3 Cover the pot and cook for 2 hours over low heat. Remove the bay leaf before serving.

Note: Cutting each cube of beef into quarters produces a moister and more delicious stew because of the increased surface that is flavored by the other ingredients. And small pieces of beef look more attractive than large chunks.

Serves 2 generously

Beef Stew 2: Beef Burgundy

Americans think of this as a dish for dinner guests; for the French, who know it as *boeuf bourguignon*, it is one of the mainstays of family cooking. Here are the essentials for *boeuf bourguignon*. Serve with Boiled New Potatoes.

1 medium onion
1 strip bacon
¾ pound stewing beef, cubed
1½ cups good red wine, preferably Burgundy

1 clove garlic, peeled and minced
bouquet garni: few sprigs fresh parsley, ¼ teaspoon dried thyme, and 1 bay leaf
salt and pepper to taste

Optional:
butter, flour, onion, whole cloves, mushrooms, small onions

1 Peel and chop the onion. Cut the bacon in small pieces and cook over medium heat in a heavy saucepan.

2 Add the beef and brown it in the bacon fat, mixing with the pieces of bacon. Add the chopped onion and let it brown.

3 Add the wine and mix well. Add all the seasonings. Cover and simmer for 2 hours. Correct the seasoning, remove the bay leaf (and cloves if used) and serve.

Note: You may add a tablespoon of butter in Step 1, a tablespoon of flour in Step 2 (sprinkled over the meat), an onion stuck with 4 cloves in Step 3, and as many tiny whole onions as you wish 25 minutes before serving. Add ½ pound sliced mushrooms 15 minutes before serving. Even without these additions, you will have a delicious beef stew.

Serves 2 generously

Beef Stew 3:
Beef with
Tea-Soaked Raisins

Here is a surprising combination—beef and tea. It produces a delicate and interesting stew that gains steadily in flavor after it is cooked. It is a perfect choice for a dinner party: cook it the day before and you will have one less thing to do on a busy day. Serve with rice or noodles.

3 large onions
3 tablespoons safflower or corn oil, divided
¾ pound stewing beef
¼ cup raisins soaked in strong tea for 2 or 3 hours

salt and pepper to taste

1 Peel and slice the onions. Over medium-high heat, heat 2 tablespoons of the oil in a large, covered skillet, add the onions and sauté for about 10 minutes, removing them when they become yellow and transferring them to a bowl.

2 Add the third tablespoon of oil, and when it sizzles, add the beef and sauté it until the cubes are browned on all sides.

3 Remove the raisins from the tea with a slotted spoon or strainer. Add the onions and the tea-soaked raisins to the beef and stir well. Reduce the heat and cover. Simmer for at least 2 hours. Correct the seasoning before serving.

Serves 2 generously

Hamburger Pie

The perfect recipe for those times when one is faced with what to do with a package of frozen hamburger meat. What follows is the basic recipe; the dish can be made more elaborate by adding a chopped, sautéed onion, ½ cup of ricotta or cottage cheese, and a good sprinkling of Parmesan cheese in Step 2. Serve with egg noodles, polenta, bulgur wheat, kasha, barley, or white or brown rice.

- 2 tablespoons butter or olive, safflower, or corn oil
- ½ pound lean ground round steak or chuck steak
- 14½-ounce can tomatoes or 3 fresh tomatoes, sliced
- 2 ounces mozzarella or Swiss cheese, sliced

- *1 teaspoon dried basil*
- *½ teaspoon dried oregano*
- *¼ teaspoon garlic powder*
- *½ teaspoon salt*
- *pepper to taste*

1 Heat the butter or oil, and when it is hot, add the meat. (If the meat you are using is frozen, cover the pan and cook over medium heat, uncovering to scrape the block of meat as it thaws and spread it over the pan as it cooks. In between, keep the pan covered so that the meat will cook faster.)

2 Spread the meat as evenly as possible over the bottom of the pan. Add the tomatoes and cheese. Sprinkle the seasonings over the surface.

3 Cover and cook gently 20 to 25 minutes.

Serves 2

Beef Liver, Venetian Style

This excellent recipe can be successfully adapted to chicken livers. Serve with Cornmeal Pudding or Fried Bread.

8 ounces beef liver, cut
   in ½-inch slices*
1 or 2 onions
3 tablespoons butter,
   divided
2 medium apples

salt and pepper to taste

1 Slice the onions and sauté them in 2 tablespoons of butter over medium-high heat.

2 Core the apples, peel them if you like, and slice them into rings. Push the onions to the side and sauté the apples for a few minutes until soft. Remove the apples from the pan.

3 Add the third tablespoon of butter to the pan, and when hot, add the liver slices; sauté for a few minutes *only*, still on medium-high heat. Season with salt and pepper. Serve the mixture of liver and onions with the apples as a garnish.

Serves 2

* See page 265 for a tip on slicing raw meat.

Sausage and Lentils

Lima beans or pintos are good substitutes for lentils in this recipe. Use Italian or Polish sausage or the Spanish chorizo if possible, as they have the best flavor, though ordinary breakfast sausage will also do. Serve with Carrot Salad.

2 cups cooked lentils, drained (page 278)
2 large sausage links
2 onions
½ cup chicken or beef stock

salt and pepper to taste

1 Cook the sausage as directed on the package—generally, by placing it in a cold skillet and proceeding as follows: prick the sausage, add an inch of water, bring it to the boil, cover the pan, reduce the heat, and cook for 15 minutes. Most of the water will have evaporated. Pour off any remaining water and the fat. Leaving the lid off, continue to cook the sausage, turning it now and then as it browns. Cut into slices.

2 Chop or slice the onions and sauté them in the same pan after removing sausage. (There ought to be enough fat left for sautéing; in fact, it would be healthy to pour off any excess—in a jar, not down the drain.)

3 Mix the sausage and onions with the lentils and stock. Heat and mix well. Season with salt and pepper.

Serves 2

POULTRY

Baked Spiced Chicken

This is a lovely recipe, and your house will become fragrant with spices as the chicken cooks. Serve with rice.

3- to 4-pound roasting
   chicken
1 tangerine, orange,
   lemon, or lime

¼ *teaspoon each ground*
   cinnamon, ground cloves,
   and garlic powder

Optional:
¼ *teaspoon any or all of*
   the following: carda-
   mom, curry powder,
   dried mint, nutmeg

Preheat the oven to 350°.

1 Remove the viscera from the cavity of the chicken and rinse the chicken under cold water, inside and out. Pat the skin dry with paper towels.

2 Place the citrus fruit in the larger cavity. Season, dusting the skin well with all the spices.

3 Place the chicken on a rack in the roasting pan. Pour 1 cup of water into the pan and bake the chicken for 1 hour to 1 hour 20 minutes, basting with the liquid in the pan 3 or 4 times during the last 30 minutes.

Note: A good rule of thumb for roasting time is about 20 minutes to a pound in a 350° oven. To test for doneness, prick the leg with a fork. If the juice is no longer pink, the chicken is done. It should be very crusty on the outside and moist inside.
Serves 4

Chicken Baked
with Sherry

The chicken in this recipe becomes beautifully glazed and succulent. Serve with buttered noodles.

3- to 4-pound roasting
  chicken
1 onion
½ cup dry sherry

salt and pepper to taste

Preheat the oven to 350°.

1 Remove the viscera from the cavity of the chicken, rinse the chicken under cold water inside and out, and pat dry with paper towels.

2 Place the chicken in a baking pan. Peel the onion and place it inside the chicken.

3 Bake for 30 minutes. Pour the sherry over the chicken and bake another 30 to 50 minutes (depending on the size of the chicken), basting from time to time. Add a bit of water if the juices seem to be drying out. Season.

Serves 4

Chicken with Garlic, or Poulet Béarnais

This dish, cooked for Henry IV of France and celebrated by the English novelist Ford Madox Ford, is simplicity itself. The effect of so much garlic is much the same as that produced by garlic soup—sweet, subtle, and interesting rather than overpowering. The stewed cloves of garlic can be eaten as if they were white beans. (See page 276 for help in peeling the garlic, although you may sharply reduce the amount if you tire or remain skeptical.) Serve with baked potatoes.

3- to 4-pound roasting chicken

2 pounds garlic cloves

salt and pepper to taste

Preheat the oven to 350°.

1 Remove the viscera from the cavity of the chicken, rinse the chicken under cold water inside and out, and pat dry with paper towels.

2 Peel the cloves of garlic and place them in the middle of the roasting pan.

3 Place the chicken *over* the bed of garlic cloves and bake for 1 to 1¼ hours, basting from time to time during the last 30 minutes. Season.

Serves 4

Baked Chicken with Lime

Use either a whole chicken, cut up, or a package of any parts you like—legs, thighs, whole quarters, breasts, or any combination. Chicken breasts may require less baking, depending on their size: split them if you are in a hurry. Serve with fresh corn or baked potatoes or Broiled Potatoes.

1 chicken, cut up
2 limes
½ tablespoon butter or
   margarine

1 clove garlic, peeled and
   minced
1 tablespoon paprika
pinch of cayenne pepper
salt to taste

Preheat the oven to 350°.

1 Wash the chicken parts and spread them in a roasting pan. Dot with butter and sprinkle with all the seasonings.

2 Squeeze the limes. Sprinkle the juice over the chicken.

3 Grate the rinds and add to the chicken. Bake for 1 hour, basting several times with the juices at the bottom of the pan. (It is best to use a baster.)

Serves 4

Baked Chicken with Sesame

Accompany this with rice and Cucumber Salad.

1 chicken, cut into 8 pieces
¾ cup soy sauce
¼ cup sugar

2 cloves garlic, peeled
1 teaspoon freshly grated ginger
3 tablespoons sesame seeds

Optional:
1 scallion

Preheat the oven to 350°.

1 Wash the chicken parts and place them in a greased casserole or oven dish.

2 Boil together the soy sauce, sugar, garlic, ginger, and sesame seeds until the sugar dissolves. Pour the mixture over the chicken.

3 Bake about 1 hour. Garnish, if you wish, with finely chopped scallion.

Serves 4

Easy Oven-Fried Chicken

This is a healthy version of fried chicken: the "batter" is low in cholesterol, and baking—with no added fat—replaces deep-fat frying. Serve with hot crusty rolls or Appalachian Corn Bread.

1 chicken cut into 8 pieces, or a package of any parts you prefer ¾ cup cornmeal corn oil	½ teaspoon dried sage ½ teaspoon garlic powder salt and pepper to taste

Preheat the oven to 350°.

1 Wash and pat the chicken dry with paper towels.

2 Place the cornmeal, seasonings, and chicken in a strong plastic or paper bag. Close securely and shake until the chicken is well coated.

3 Brush or pour a thin layer of oil in the baking pan. Place the coated chicken parts on the oiled pan. Bake for 1 hour, turning once in the course of baking.

Serves 4

Chicken Breast with Hearts of Palm

The flavor of the hearts of palm gives this dish its distinction. Appropriate for the grandest occasions, it could hardly be simpler. Serve with buttered noodles.

2 boneless chicken breasts, split

3 tablespoons butter or palm oil, if available

1 can hearts of palm, drained

1 clove garlic, peeled and minced

salt and pepper to taste

2 tablespoons minced fresh parsley

Optional:
3 tablespoons light cream

1 Remove all skin and fat from the chicken. Wash and dry.

2 Melt the butter (or heat the oil) over medium heat. Add the garlic and sauté the breasts, turning once, until brown. Lower the heat and continue to cook 10–12 minutes.

3 When the chicken is almost done, sauté the hearts of palm in the same pan. Season with salt and pepper and remove to a warmed platter. Arrange the hearts of palm over the chicken. Sprinkle with parsley. If you wish, add the cream to the juices in the pan. Stir well and heat through. Spoon over the chicken and hearts of palm.

Serves 2 generously

Lemon Chicken

This is a memorable chicken dish. Serve with boiled potatoes, a green vegetable and/or salad.

2 tablespoons butter or olive, safflower, or corn oil
1 chicken, cut into 8 pieces
4 lemons, divided

salt and pepper to taste

Optional:
⅓ cup light cream

1 Use a skillet large enough for all the pieces to fit without overlapping. Heat the butter or oil and sauté the chicken over medium-high heat, turning each piece so that all sides brown lightly.

2 Cut up 2 of the lemons into small slices and place them over the chicken. Cover the pan. Simmer for 30 minutes or until done.

3 Squeeze the other 2 lemons and pour the juice over the chicken. If you wish, add the cream and mix well. Don't allow the sauce to boil. Season before serving.

Serves 4

Chicken with Sausage

For a very ample one-pot dinner, add as many of the following as you like, allowing 2 vegetables per person: peeled potatoes, onions, whole peeled carrots, and diagonally cut stalks of celery. Place them over the chicken at the beginning of cooking time.

1 Italian sausage, cut into thin slices
1 chicken, cut into 8 pieces
8-ounce can tomato sauce

½ teaspoon dried sage

1 Heat a skillet and add a slice of sausage pushing it about until the surface of the pan is well greased. Fry the remaining sausage slices and pour off as much fat as possible into a jar (to avoid clogging the kitchen drain).

2 Place the chicken parts over the fried sausage slices and add the tomato sauce and sage.

3 Cover and cook gently for 1 hour, occasionally mixing the sausage slices and chicken.

Serves 4

West African Peanut Soup, or Domada

Although called a soup, this is more like a stew and should be served over rice. A version of this dish survives in Virginia peanut soup.

1 chicken, cut into 8 pieces
½–1 cup chunky peanut butter
6-ounce can tomato paste

cayenne pepper to taste*
salt and pepper to taste

1 Place the chicken in 3 cups of water. Bring to a boil, lower the heat, cover, and simmer 20 minutes.

2 Add the peanut butter to the pot, mix well, and continue to simmer another 30 minutes, or until the liquid thickens.

3 Add the tomato paste and continue to cook 15 to 20 minutes, stirring well from time to time. Season and serve.

Optional: To expand the stew, you can add sautéed chopped vegetables (onions, peppers, celery, cauliflower, cabbage) to the pot just after you incorporate the tomato paste in Step 3. Allow 1 cup vegetables per serving.

Serves 4

* Start with a pinch and increase amount gradually to taste.

Chicken Paprika

This recipe dispenses with the sautéing usually required in making this traditional Hungarian dish. Long simmering develops the flavor in this version. Serve with noodles.

1 **chicken, cut into 8 pieces**	1 *clove garlic, peeled and*
8-ounce can tomato sauce	*chopped*
3 **tablespoons sour cream**	2 *tablespoons paprika*
	salt and pepper to taste

1 Place the chicken parts in a skillet or saucepan. Pour the tomato sauce over them.

2 Add the spices and cover. Simmer slowly for 1½ hours.

3 Remove from heat, stir in sour cream and return to heat for a few minutes but do not allow to boil.

Serves 4

Buffalo Chicken Wings

This is the Durkee Company's official recipe for baked chicken wings. It is much less time-consuming to bake than to fry the wings and certainly less fattening. Serve with plenty of paper napkins, French-Fried Sweet Potatoes, and a salad.

2½ pounds chicken wings (12 to 15 wings)
6 tablespoons Durkee RedHot! Sauce*
½ stick butter or margarine, melted

Preheat the oven to 325°.

1 Cut each wing in two at the joint. Discard the tips; wash and pat the wings dry with paper towels.

2 Place the wings in a bowl. Combine the hot sauce and melted butter and pour over the wings. Cover and marinate in the refrigerator 3 hours or longer, turning several times.

3 Transfer the wings and sauce to a heatproof dish and bake them, uncovered, 30 minutes. Just before serving, preheat the broiler and broil 3 to 4 inches from the source of heat for 4 to 5 minutes on each side, turning until the wings are brown and crisp.

Makes 24 to 30 pieces

* For hotter wings, use ¾ cup.

Chicken Livers with Artichoke Hearts

A fast sauté, and a very good one. Serve with rice.

1 pound chicken livers
9-ounce package frozen artichoke hearts, defrosted
3 tablespoons butter or olive oil

1 small clove garlic, peeled and minced
¼ teaspoon paprika
salt and pepper to taste

Optional:
1 scallion, finely chopped
2 tablespoons sour cream

1 Rinse the chicken livers and pat them dry with paper towels. Cut them in half. Drain the defrosted artichokes well.

2 Heat the butter and garlic in a skillet over medium-high heat and sauté the artichokes briefly, 2 to 3 minutes.

3 Push them to the side and sauté the chicken livers, 3 to 5 minutes. Season with paprika, salt, and pepper and mix the livers and artichokes well, sautéing another 2 minutes. Garnish, if you wish, with sour cream and chopped scallion.

Serves 4

FOUR-INGREDIENT RECIPES

Chicken Nuggets in Peanut Sauce

If you are pressed for time, omit the marinating in preparing the chicken and use the marinade merely as a sauce.

1 medium onion
2 boneless chicken breasts, split
3 tablespoons soy sauce
2 heaping tablespoons crunchy peanut butter

2 *cloves garlic, peeled and minced*
½ *teaspoon chili powder*
salt and pepper to taste

Optional:
1 *tablespoon toasted sesame seeds*

1 Chop the onion. Cut the chicken into nugget-sized pieces and place in a small broiling pan.

2 Place the onion in a saucepan. Add the soy sauce and peanut butter plus ½ cup water and the seasonings. Mix well and bring to a boil. Simmer 5 minutes.

3 Pour the marinade over the chicken. Let stand for 1 to 2 hours, turning from time to time. Broil in the marinade for 10 to 15 minutes, turning several times. If you wish, garnish with sesame seeds before serving.

Note: The sauce made in Step 2 can also be mixed with ¾ pound ground beef and either stir-fried for 5 minutes or shaped into patties and broiled for 10 minutes.

Serves 4

Chicken Breast and Eggplant

According to the friend who first gave it to me, this recipe "tastes complicated" even though it's not. Accompany it with noodles.

1 small eggplant (about ¾ pound)

6 tablespoons olive oil, divided

2 boneless chicken breasts, split

3 tablespoons dry sherry

1 clove garlic, peeled and minced

2 tablespoons minced fresh parsley

salt and pepper to taste

1 Cut the eggplant in round slices, about ⅜ inch thick. Leave the skin on if you like.*

2 Heat 3 tablespoons of the oil in a skillet over medium-high heat, add the eggplant, and sauté until brown. Turn the slices, add the garlic, and sauté until the second side browns. Remove the slices and place on paper towels to absorb the excess oil.

3 In the same pan, still over medium-high heat, add the remaining 3 tablespoons of oil, and when the oil is hot, sauté the chicken, turning once, cooking each side 4 to 5 minutes. Place the cooked eggplant slices over the chicken breasts, covering them completely. Add the sherry and 2 tablespoons of water, cover the pan, and lower the heat. Cook gently for 5 minutes. Season, sprinkle with parsley, and serve.

Serves 2 generously

* See page 267 for preliminary salting and rinsing to draw out the bitterness in eggplant.

Stewed Chicken with Beer and Olives

The friend who gave me this recipe uses a crockpot, placing the four ingredients in it before she leaves the house at 8 A.M. When she returns at 6:30 P.M., the chicken is ready for the family dinner, to be supplemented with kasha and a salad. I've adapted the recipe for those who don't own crockpots. As to what to do with the other half can of beer, either drink it or double the recipe.

1 **chicken, cut into 8 pieces**
½ **can beer**
½ **of 6-ounce can tomato paste**
½ **of 3-ounce jar green olives stuffed with pimientos**

¼ *teaspoon dried oregano*
¼ *teaspoon dried basil*
salt and pepper to taste

1 Rinse the chicken parts and place them in a skillet with a close-fitting lid.

2 Mix the beer and tomato paste and pour over the chicken. Drain the olives and add to the chicken.

3 Bring to a boil, then cover, lower heat, and simmer for 1 hour.

Serves 4

Roast Duckling

Not a very difficult undertaking, but a very glamoro[us]
During the last half hour of roasting, when you begin to
baste the duckling, place sliced cored apples or canned
apricot halves on an oiled oven dish and pour a few spoons
of the honey mixture over the fruit. Bake while the duck is
roasting, and serve with the bird.

**4-pound duckling, either
fresh or frozen and
thawed
½ cup soy sauce
½ cup honey
½ cup apple cider or other
fruit juice**

*½ teaspoon ground ginger
salt and pepper to taste*

Preheat the oven to 350°.

1 Remove the viscera from the cavity of the duck, rinse the
duck well under cold water, pat dry, and place it on a rack
that fits your oven pan.

2 Roast for 1½ hours. As the duck cooks and fat accumulates
in the pan, remove as much as you can with a large baster,
every 15 minutes or so. This cuts down on the amount of fat
you and your guests will consume and means that your oven
need not be cleaned before you can use it again.

3 Mix the soy sauce, honey, apple cider, and seasonings and
pour over the duck. Bake another 30 minutes, basting every
10 minutes.

Note: In choosing a duck, look for smaller rather than larger
ones: the difference in weight means more fat rather than
more meat. Since duck is very rich, a 4-pounder should serve
4. For hearty appetites, cook 2 ducks.

Serves 4

FISH AND SHELLFISH

Scallops in the Shell

These simply prepared scallops look especially impressive served in real scallop shells, accompanied by Rice Pilaf and a salad.

½ pound scallops
¼ cup dry vermouth
1 tablespoon butter

¼ teaspoon dried rose-
    mary or thyme
salt and pepper to taste

Preheat the oven to 350°.

1 If the scallops are large (sea scallops), dice them; bay scallops need no cutting. Divide between two (or more) shells or gratin dishes.

2 Pour the vermouth over the scallops and dot them with butter. Season with rosemary or thyme, salt, and pepper.

3 Bake 10 to 15 minutes.

Serves 2 as a main dish or 4 as an appetizer

Broiled Shrimp, or Scampi

This standard restaurant dish can easily be prepared at home if you are willing to take the trouble to shell and devein the shrimp. Serve with hot rolls, rice, and Coleslaw.

1 pound fresh shrimp,
    unshelled
1 large lemon
¼ cup olive oil

2–3 *cloves garlic, peeled*
    and minced
salt and pepper to taste
few sprigs fresh parsley

Preheat the broiler.

1 Shell and devein the shrimp.* Wash well.

2 Arrange the shrimp on a broiling pan. Cut the lemon in half and squeeze one half. Mix the juice and the garlic with the olive oil and pour over the shrimp. Season with salt and pepper.

3 Broil 3 to 4 minutes on each side, basting twice. Keep an eye on the shrimp as they broil, turning them so that they are all equally coated and separate from one another. When they are pink, they are ready. Serve with slices of lemon from the remaining half lemon and a few sprigs of parsley.

Serves 2

* To shell and devein shrimp, remove the legs and slide off the shell. Using a small, sharp knife cut away the dark intestinal vein that runs along the back of the shrimp.

Shrimp in Beer

The flavor of the shrimp gains a good deal from the beer. Serve with fresh homemade mayonnaise (see page 174), mixed with any of the following: finely chopped capers, scallions, parsley, or tarragon. Serve with Irish Soda Bread or hot French bread, rice, and a green salad.

1 lemon
1 can beer
1 pound fresh shrimp,
   unshelled

1 small bay leaf
2 cloves garlic, peeled
½ teaspoon salt
pepper to taste

1 Squeeze the lemon. In a saucepan combine the lemon juice with the beer and seasonings and bring to a good boil.

2 Add the shrimp, cover the pot, and bring to a boil again. At this point, uncover the pot and cook until the shrimp turns pink—no more than a few minutes.

3 Drain the shrimp. Allow to cool. Shell and devein the shrimp (see page 98 for instructions).

Serves 2

Grilled Fish with Mustard

This recipe works best with the more strongly flavored fish like bluefish, mackerel, and herring. Serve with Mashed Potatoes.

1 pound fish, cleaned
   and split
½ lime

2 tablespoons Dijon
   mustard
salt and pepper to taste

Preheat the broiler.

1 Rinse and dry the fish and place it in a broiling pan, skin side up.

2 Cook for 1 or 2 minutes. Turn the fish, spread with mustard on the flesh side, and return to the broiler.

3 Grill for another 5 minutes or so, until the fish flakes easily. Squeeze lime juice over the fish and season with salt and pepper before serving.

Serves 2

Baked Fish Fillets with Mushrooms

In this recipe the fish is placed on a bed of mushrooms and herbs and protected from drying out by the layer of bread crumbs covering it. You may want to sprinkle a few drops of lemon juice over the fish before adding the bread crumbs. Serve with Baked Potatoes and Fresh Beets with Dill.

½ pound mushrooms
2 portions flounder, blue-fish, haddock, halibut, trout, salmon, or sole
3 tablespoons bread crumbs

small handful fresh parsley, chopped
½ clove garlic, peeled and chopped
1 tablespoon chopped fresh chives or scallion
¼ teaspoon dried marjoram
salt and pepper to taste

Optional:
2 tablespoons grated Parmesan cheese
1–2 tablespoons butter

Preheat the oven to 350°.

1 Clean and slice the mushrooms (see page 148). Mix them with all the seasonings and lay out half the mixture on an oiled baking pan just large enough for the fish.

2 Place the fish over the mushrooms and herbs and cover it with the other half of the mixture.

3 Sprinkle with bread crumbs. (If you like, they may be mixed with grated Parmesan cheese and/or dotted with butter.) Bake 20 to 30 minutes.

Serves 2

Steamed Fish with Black Bean Sauce

This traditional Chinese cooking method is appropriate for any firm-fleshed fish. Sea bass is excellent prepared this way, as are red snapper, white perch, rainbow trout, or Spanish mackerel; fillets may be used as well. Allow ½ pound of whole fish and ¼ to ⅓ pound of fillets per person. Serve with rice.

Any small whole fish, scaled and washed, or 2 portions fish fillets
1½ tablespoons fermented black bean sauce* per pound of fish
1 tablespoon slivered fresh ginger per pound of fish

Optional:
1 teaspoon dry sherry per pound of fish
1 scallion per pound of fish, cut into 1-inch lengths

1 Place the fish in a heatproof serving dish. If you are using a whole fish, score it lightly 3 or 4 times on both sides.

2 Spread the bean sauce over the fish and sprinkle with ginger (and scallions as well as sherry, if you wish).

3 Steam the fish by placing the dish over boiling water in a large covered pot or wok. (I use a jar lid to keep the platter elevated over the boiling water.) Steam 8 to 10 minutes, or until the flesh flakes easily and is no longer translucent. A whole fish is done when the eyes go completely white and—this is not a point for the squeamish—are loose enough to pop out.

Serves 2

* Some Oriental groceries do not stock fermented black bean sauce, though virtually all such stores stock the fermented beans: the sauce is prepared by soaking and mashing the beans in enough soy sauce to make a wet—and not very smooth—paste.

Fresh Trout

When trout is absolutely fresh, there are few foods that can surpass it. Defrosted frozen trout can also be used in this recipe, as can any other small whole fresh fish. This is good served with Sautéed Red Radishes and Rice Pilaf.

2 small trout, cleaned with gills and heads removed
2–3 tablespoons cornmeal
2 tablespoons butter or peanut, safflower, or corn oil (preferably a mixture)*

salt and pepper to taste

Optional:
½ lemon, cut in wedges

1 Rinse and dry the trout.

2 Heat the butter and/or oil over medium-high heat while you dredge the fish in cornmeal. (Some cooks dip the fish in milk before dredging so that crumbs adhere better.)

3 Sauté the fish 3 to 5 minutes on each side over medium-high heat, turning carefully, until well browned and the flesh is firm and flakes easily. Season with salt and pepper and serve. If you wish, garnish with wedges of lemon.

Serves 2

* The mixture of oil with butter will keep the butter from burning.

Sautéed Fish Fillets

For those who do not have easy access to fresh fish and must rely on supermarket frozen fish, this recipe does what it can to give frozen fillets a pleasant and distinctive flavor. Serve with Spinach Bhurta or steamed spinach and Appalachian Corn Bread.

1 strip bacon
1 onion
1 pound fish fillets, thawed

salt and pepper to taste

Optional:
1 tablespoon Herb Butter (page 190) or 1 tablespoon butter

1 Cut the bacon into 1-inch pieces. Chop the onion.

2 Fry the bacon pieces, pouring off as much of the fat as you can. When the bacon is almost crisp, add the onion to the pan, sautéing it briefly.

3 Move the bacon and onions to the side, place the fish fillets gently in the pan, and sauté them briefly over medium heat, a few minutes on each side. Mound the bacon and onions over the fillets, lower the heat, put the lid on the pan, and cook a few more minutes, until the fish loses its transparency. Garnish with butter if you wish.

Serves 2 generously

Simple Salmon Timbale

A timbale is simply a custard containing vegetables, meat, fish, or cheese. This one, a light, delicate baked salmon with a definite dill flavor, can be assembled in a few minutes; baking time can be as short as 10 minutes if you use a 10-inch quiche pan, longer for a deeper dish. Serve with Steamed Cucumber and Blue Cheese (page 129) and pumpernickel bread.

15½-ounce can salmon
1 cup creamed cottage cheese
1 egg

½ teaspoon picante sauce or few drops Tabasco
½ teaspoon dried dillweed
1 teaspoon dried parsley or small handful fresh parsley
salt and pepper to taste

Optional:
2 tablespoons sour cream or yogurt

Preheat the oven to 350°.

1 Drain the salmon.

2 Place all the ingredients and seasonings in a blender or processor and blend well.

3 Pour the mixture into a greased quiche pan or deep pie plate. Bake 10 minutes for a 10-inch pan or 15 to 20 minutes for an 8-inch pan. Cut into wedges and garnish each wedge with 1 tablespoon sour cream or yogurt if desired.

Serves 3

EGGS AND CHEESE

Interesting Scrambled Eggs

If you're tired of scrambled eggs, try these.

4 eggs
1½ ounces cream cheese*
  or ½ cup cottage cheese
1–2 tablespoons butter

½ teaspoon dried chives,
  dillweed, tarragon,
  chervil, or marjoram
salt and pepper to taste

1 Lightly beat together the eggs, cream cheese or cottage cheese, and herbs.

2 Melt the butter over medium-high heat and when the foam subsides, pour the mixture in.

3 Stir from time to time until set. Season.

Serves 2

  * Half of a 3-ounce package.

Frittata

This traditional Italian way of preparing eggs is ideal for people who think they can't make an omelet. It is far less perilous because very little can go wrong. Moreover, you can cook a much larger number of eggs at the same time, serving them in wedges, as you would a pie. Just be sure to use a cast-iron pan. Frittata can be eaten cold on picnics, or it makes an excellent sandwich.

4 eggs
2 tablespoons olive oil
3 tablespoons grated
　　Parmesan cheese

¼ teaspoon salt
pepper to taste

1 Salt the eggs and beat until fluffy. Heat the olive oil in a pan over medium-high heat. (If you are using an electric stove, turn on another burner to low heat.)

2 When the oil is hot, pour in the eggs and shake the Parmesan cheese over the surface. Reduce the heat to low (or move the pan to the low burner).

3 Allow the eggs to sit undisturbed in the pan until the edges are cooked. Cover for a few minutes or until the surface is no longer runny, or, better yet, place the frittata under the broiler for a few minutes.

Serves 2

Some Suggested Fillings

¼ to ½ cup of any of the following:

    chopped vegetables—sautéed green or red pepper, sautéed onion, sautéed mushrooms, cooked drained spinach, cooked peas, cooked potatoes

grated hard cheese—Swiss, Cheddar, provolone, or Parmesan

ricotta cheese

crumbled feta cheese

bean or alfalfa sprouts, chopped and mixed with a few drops of soy sauce

nuts—chopped pecans, walnuts, almonds, hazelnuts, or pine nuts

flaked cooked crabmeat

slivered cooked ham or cooked pork

Eggs with Ham or Asparagus in Cheese Sauce

This is a good recipe to celebrate spring when fresh asparagus is abundant. However, with or without asparagus, this is a dependable dish for lunch, brunch, or dinner. Serve with little new potatoes.

4 eggs
¾ cup cheese sauce
  (page 181)
¼ cup diced cooked ham
  or ½ pound cooked
  asparagus, or both

salt and pepper to taste

1 Hard-cook the eggs according to the rule (page 276). Peel and slice the eggs carefully and season with salt and pepper.

2 Make the sauce.

3 Add the ham or asparagus or both. Heat gently in the hot sauce and pour everything over the sliced eggs.

Serves 2

Ricotta Pie

This baked custard depends for its delicacy on the freshness of the ingredients. It makes a nice lunch accompanied by fresh sliced tomatoes sprinkled with basil.

1 **pound ricotta cheese**
4 **eggs**
¼ **cup grated Parmesan cheese**

2 *sprigs fresh parsley*
¼ *teaspoon freshly grated nutmeg*
⅓ *teaspoon salt*
pepper to taste

Preheat the oven to 350°.

1 Mix all the ingredients well in a food processor or with a beater. (Chop the parsley sprigs if you use a beater.)

2 Pour into an oiled 8-inch quiche pan or a 9-inch pie plate.

3 Bake 20-25 minutes, or until golden brown and puffy. It is done when a knife inserted in the center comes out clean.

Note: For variety, add ½ cup cooked vegetables (peppers, mushrooms or broccoli are good) to the basic mixture in Step 1.

Serves 2 generously

Fried Cheese, or Saganaki

In making this traditional Greek dish, try to find imported Kasseri cheese, which is made with goat's milk and salt and sold in Greek specialty shops. Kasseri seems to keep its shape better than any other kind of cheese, and the imported variety does better than the domestic. Greek restaurants don't need to worry when the cheese loses its shape because the portions are prepared and served in individual little pans which make it unnecessary to transfer the melted cheese to a plate. Do the best you can, and even if you find yourself with a puddle of melted cheese, it will be so delicious no one will object. (A Teflon-coated pan will help to keep the cheese from sticking.)

2 tablespoons olive oil
1 portion Kasseri cheese
   (about 2 x 2 x 1 inches)
2 tablespoons flour

Optional:
few drops lemon juice

1 Heat the olive oil; meanwhile wet all sides of the cheese under cold water and dust with flour on all sides.

2 When the oil is *very* hot (sizzling), put the cheese in the pan. Lower the heat and allow the cheese to fry 3 to 4 minutes, watching it carefully. Do not cover the pan.

3 Turn the cheese with a spatula and fry another minute or two. Serve with fresh pita and a squeeze of lemon juice if desired.

Serves 1

Welsh Rarebit

This is a Welsh rarebit for people who like the taste of beer. If you're not one of them, you may want to substitute ¼ cup milk for the beer.

½ pound sharp Cheddar cheese
2 eggs
¼ can beer

⅛ teaspoon paprika
½ teaspoon Worcester-shire sauce
1–2 drops Tabasco sauce
salt and pepper to taste

1 Shave or grate the cheese and heat it in a double boiler until thoroughly melted, stirring occasionally.

2 Beat the eggs well and add the seasonings and beer. Beat the mixture into the melted cheese little by little. Stir all the while.

3 Serve hot on freshly made toast.

Serves 2 generously

FOUR-INGREDIENT RECIPES

Eggs in Burgundy

These remarkable eggs can be served with crusty French bread, Fried Bread (page 198), or Mashed Potatoes (page 137). Perhaps a chef for one of the Kings of France devised this recipe, since so much Burgundy is lavished on 4 eggs. In any case, it is eminently suitable for guests at lunch or brunch.

4 medium onions
2 tablespoons butter
½ bottle Burgundy
4 eggs

salt and pepper to taste

1 Peel and slice the onions (see page 269 for help with onions). Heat the butter in a skillet, and when it is hot, add the onions and sauté them.

2 When the onions are light yellow, add the wine and cook slowly for 30 minutes, uncovered.

3 When the onions are thoroughly done and the liquid nearly evaporated, break the eggs one by one into the sauce, being careful to keep the yolks whole. Leave the eggs undisturbed in the sauce, where they will cook in a few minutes. Be sure not to turn the eggs, in case you are tempted.

Serves 2

Scrambled Eggs and Smoked Salmon, or Lox

This recipe can be used with confidence for any boneless smoked fish—and it is also highly recommended for salami.

2 ounces smoked salmon
4 eggs
1 medium onion
3 tablespoons butter, divided

1 Cut the smoked salmon into thin slices. Break the eggs in a bowl and beat. Peel and chop the onion.

2 Heat 2 tablespoons of butter in a skillet, add the onion and sauté over medium-high heat until yellow. Push the onion to the side of the pan and add the smoked salmon; sauté for 2 or 3 minutes.

3 Add the third tablespoon of butter, and when it sizzles, add the eggs. Lower the heat and stir everything together. Keep stirring until the eggs are cooked as you like them.

Serves 2

Baked Soufflé-Omelet with Mushrooms and Feta Cheese

Just the thing for a late-night supper. Use a cast-iron skillet or one that can be placed in the oven.

4 eggs
¼ pound mushrooms
2 tablespoons butter, divided
4 ounces feta cheese, crumbled (or sharp cheese, grated)

salt and pepper to taste

Preheat the oven to 400°.

1 Separate the eggs (see page 274), first beating the whites until stiff and then beating the yolks. (See page 275 for these techniques.)

2 Clean and slice the mushrooms. Melt 1 tablespoon of the butter in a skillet over medium-high heat, and when the foam subsides, add the mushrooms and sauté them 7 to 8 minutes, or until brown. When they are done, remove from heat and allow to cool. Mix the mushrooms with the beaten egg yolks. Fold in the whites.

3 Heat the second tablespoon of butter in the skillet. Pour in the egg mixture and sprinkle the cheese over the top. When the mixture begins to harden and retract slightly from the sides of the pan, put the skillet in the oven and bake 10 to 15 minutes, or until the top is browned. Season with salt and pepper and cut into wedges.

Serves 3

Cottage Cheese Pancakes

This recipe was reinvented by a friend in search of the pancakes of her childhood. These are the proportions she finally decided were right. These pancakes are good served with sour cream or sprinkled with sugar (or both) or with yogurt sprinkled with a little sugar and cardamom.

1 **cup small-curd creamy cottage cheese**
2 **tablespoons flour**
2 **eggs**
3 **tablespoons butter**

salt to taste

1 Mix together the cottage cheese, flour, eggs, and salt to make a batter. The batter will be lumpy but do not be concerned.

2 Melt the butter in a skillet over medium heat, and when it is hot, pour in just enough batter to make little pancakes, about 2 inches in diameter.

3 Turn the pancakes only once, allowing them to brown on both sides. Serve hot.

Serves 2 generously

Cheese Timbale

When this filling is used with a pie crust, it is known as quiche. This recipe, if followed exactly, will turn out with a lovely crustlike effect on the bottom. The Dijon mustard imparts an unusual tang.

¼ pound Swiss cheese
1½ tablespoons flour
3 eggs
1 cup milk or light or
   heavy cream

1 teaspoon Dijon mustard
salt and pepper to taste

Preheat the oven to 350°.

1 Grease an 8-inch quiche pan or a deep pie plate. Grate the cheese coarsely or cut it into small pieces.

2 Dredge the cheese with flour and try to cover the bottom of the pan or plate as evenly as possible with the floured cheese.

3 Beat the eggs. Mix the eggs, milk or cream, and seasonings, stirring well, and pour over the cheese, covering it completely. Bake 45 minutes, or until a knife inserted in the center emerges clean. (If you use a 10-inch quiche pan, allow 30 minutes for baking.)

Note: To make a Ham Timbale, add ¼ cup chopped ham in Step 3. To make a Spinach Timbale, add ½ cup cooked chopped spinach, being careful to press out as much of the liquid as possible. For other vegetable timbales, sauté ½ cup thawed frozen artichoke hearts, broccoli florets, or sliced zucchini and add in Step 3.

Serves 2 generously

Camper's Meal-in-One

Even if you've "nothing" on the kitchen shelves or the refrigerator, you're likely to have these ingredients. This is an old standby for campers, needing only a skillet and a spatula or a tablespoon. The result is a very ample meal. You may, of course, substitute ground beef for the eggs, but the cooking time will be longer.

4 eggs
2 medium onions
2 medium potatoes
3 tablespoons olive, saf-
    flower, or corn oil

salt and pepper to taste

Optional:
¼ *teaspoon curry powder*
    or caraway seeds

1 Beat the eggs.

2 Peel and slice the onions. Scrub and slice the potatoes thinly (peel them if you prefer).

3 Heat the oil in a skillet, add the onions and potatoes together and sauté 10 minutes, or until the potatoes begin to brown. Add the beaten eggs and seasonings and stir until cooked, 2 to 3 minutes.

VEGETABLES

Steamed Vegetables

The following recipe provides a general guideline for steaming a variety of vegetables (see Note below for approximate cooking times).

½ pound vegetables
1 tablespoon butter, margarine, or olive oil
few drops good wine vinegar (preferably tarragon vinegar) or lemon juice

¼ teaspoon dried dill, chervil, tarragon, chives, or chopped fresh parsley
salt and pepper to taste

1 Trim and wash the vegetables, peeling where necessary.

2 Place the vegetable steamer* in a saucepan with a tightly fitting lid. Add ½ inch of water, place the vegetables in the steamer, and cover.

3 Bring to a boil, lower the heat, and steam until the vegetables turn a lovely bright green. Other kinds of vegetables should be steamed until just tender. Remove the vegetables and toss with butter or oil, and vinegar or lemon juice, as well as the seasonings.

Note: Steam whole green beans for 7 minutes; broccoli, 8 to 10 minutes; cauliflower (broken into florets), about 7 minutes; green or red peppers (sliced into thin strips), about 8 minutes; small zucchini (sliced lengthwise once), 7 to 8 minutes; asparagus, 7 to 10 minutes; whole leeks (cut crosswise), 15 to 18 minutes; small Brussels sprouts, 10 to 12 minutes; snow peas, 2 to 3 minutes.

Serves 2

* Steamers can be found in most supermarkets and hardware stores.

Asparagus with Cheese

There are many ways of preparing asparagus—boiling in a large amount of water, boiling in a few inches of water, steaming in a vertical asparagus cooker, laying the asparagus down on a conventional steaming rack, etc. Feeling runs high in this matter, and you may like to try more than one method before you adopt a position.

¾ pound asparagus
2 tablespoons butter
2 tablespoons grated
  Parmesan or Romano
  cheese

salt and pepper to taste

Preheat the oven to 400°.

1 Wash the asparagus well or peel it, as some people prefer to do. Cut off or snap off the tough white ends of the stalks. Steam or boil 10 minutes (less if the stalks are thin), or until tender. Do *not* overcook: in other words, do not allow the asparagus to become a dull green.

2 Drain well and place the asparagus in a greased baking dish, dotting with butter and grated cheese. Season with salt and pepper.

3 Bake for 10 minutes, or until the grated cheese browns slightly.

Serves 2

Fresh Beets with Dill

Here is a refreshing vegetable for hot weather. If you cook two bunches at the same time, you'll be able to produce beet soup (borscht) for the next meal (see recipe page 37). Beets prepared in the following way are incomparably better than canned or bottled beets.

1 bunch small to medium beets
2–3 tablespoons wine vinegar
1 tablespoon olive oil

1 teaspoon dried dillweed
salt and pepper to taste

1 Cut away the beets from their stems. Scrub the beets well, and do not peel.

2 Put them in cold water to cover and bring to a boil. Boil 30 to 50 minutes. (Boiling time depends a good deal on the age and size of the beets.) Pierce them with a fork. If they are easily pierced, they are done. Remove the cooked beets from the liquid and plunge them into cold water. Save as much of the beet liquid as you want (at least 2 cups if you plan on borscht for two the next day).

3 Peel the cooled beets. Slice or dice them, and add the vinegar, oil, and seasonings. Toss and refrigerate for 2 to 3 hours.

Serves 2

Broccoli with Garlic and Nuts

This is the most delicious way of cooking broccoli I know, and it is really very simple. Use a cast-iron skillet.

¾ pound broccoli, washed and trimmed
3 tablespoons olive oil
3 tablespoons chopped pecans, walnuts, almonds, cashews, or whole pine nuts

2 large cloves garlic, peeled and chopped
salt and pepper to taste

1 Separate the stalks from the florets. Slice the stalks in thin discs. Cut the florets into bite-sized pieces.

2 Heat the oil over medium-high heat, and when it is hot, sauté the chopped garlic and sliced stalks for 5 minutes. If the garlic seems to be in danger of burning, remove it. Add the florets to the pan.

3 Reduce the heat to medium-low, add a few drops of water, and cover the pan. Stir the broccoli from time to time, cooking about 10 minutes or until it is tender (very shortly after it changes color). Add the nuts the last 5 minutes, stir, and season. Serve on a platter.

Note: By adding 1 cup cream and 1 cup chicken stock to this recipe you can have an excellent pasta sauce—enough for 1 pound of pasta.

Serves 2

Brussels Sprouts
with Fennel

It was once suggested that Satan offered Eve not an apple but a Brussels sprout. This vegetable, a likely candidate for the root of all evil when it is boiled until it is a yellowish green, can be redeemed in the following way.

½ pound tiny Brussels
    sprouts*
1 tablespoon olive oil
1 tablespoon butter

1 *small clove garlic,*
    peeled and chopped
¼ *teaspoon fennel seeds*
salt and pepper to taste

1 Discard the outer leaves of the sprouts, cut off the stems, and wash.

2 Steam by the rule on page 121, or parboil until just tender (about 10 to 12 minutes). Drain well.

3 Heat the oil and butter in a skillet and sauté the sprouts rapidly over medium-high heat for 3 to 4 minutes, adding the garlic and fennel. Season before serving.

Serves 2

 * The smaller the better because the more surface they present to the oil, butter, and seasonings, the better they will taste.

Cooked Grated Cabbage

This is particularly good in winter, served with any kind of potatoes and with eggs cooked any way you like.

1 small green cabbage or
  ½ medium cabbage
¼ cup lean cooked ham or
  cleaned mushrooms
4 tablespoons bacon fat
  or peanut oil, divided

½ teaspoon caraway seeds
1 teaspoon paprika
salt and pepper to taste

Optional:
2 tablespoons sour cream

1 Remove and discard the outer leaves of the cabbage. Shred the cabbage in a processor or by hand, using the coarse side of a grater. Dice the ham or chop the mushrooms.

2 Over medium-high heat, heat 2 tablespoons of the bacon fat or oil in a skillet with a tightly fitting cover.

3 Sauté the ham or mushrooms for 5 minutes and remove from the pan to a bowl. Add the other 2 tablespoons of bacon fat or oil to the skillet and sauté the cabbage for 8 to 10 minutes. Add the ham or mushrooms and mix well. Reduce the heat and cover for 3 to 5 minutes, until the cabbage is tender but crisp. Season to taste. Garnish with sour cream, if you wish.

Serves 4

Glazed Carrots

This recipe can easily be multiplied for a large number of guests (easily if you have a food processor, that is, and a 12½-inch skillet, which is large enough to cook 3 pounds of carrots at once). Since the flavor of carrots is not nearly as variable as that of, say, eggplant or zucchini, this dish is very dependable for parties.

½ pound carrots

2–3 tablespoons butter, divided

2–3 tablespoons brown sugar or maple syrup

salt to taste

1 Pare or scrape the carrots, then wash and shred them, using a food processor or the coarse side of a grater.

2 Heat half the butter in a skillet, and when sizzling, add the carrots. After a moment or two, stir, then let the mass rest for another moment before stirring again. Continue in this way until the carrots have cooked about 5 minutes.

3 Add the brown sugar or syrup and the remaining butter. Stir until the sugar dissolves and the butter melts. The carrots should be well coated. Salt lightly before serving.

Serves 2

Braised Celery

If there seems to be nothing left in the refrigerator but a few stalks of celery, here is a way to rescue them. If the celery is limp, soak it in ice water for an hour and then proceed with the recipe.

4 celery stalks
2 tablespoons butter
½ cup light cream or milk

½ *teaspoon paprika*
salt and pepper to taste

1 Wash the celery, discarding any damaged stalks or ends. Dry the stalks with paper towels and cut them into thin slices on the diagonal.

2 Melt the butter in the skillet and sauté the celery over medium heat for about 5 minutes. Season with paprika, salt, and pepper.

3 Add the cream or milk, mix well, and cover. Reduce the heat, and heat through for 2 to 3 minutes, stirring well. Do not allow the mixture to boil. The celery should still be crisp. Correct the seasoning.

Serves 2

Steamed Cucumbers and Blue Cheese

If you like cooked cucumbers, you may especially like this recipe. If you've never tried them, you may be tempted by the sheer speed and ease of preparation offered here. The brief steaming of the cucumbers leaves them still fresh and crisp, and the simple and savory blue cheese sauce does a good deal for their flavor.

2 cucumbers
1 teaspoon butter, at room temperature
3 tablespoons crumbled blue cheese

¼ teaspoon dried savory or marjoram
salt and pepper to taste

1 Peel and slice the cucumbers.

2 Place the slices in a vegetable steamer, cover, and steam 3 to 4 minutes, or until almost tender. Transfer to a serving bowl.

3 Add the butter, blue cheese, and seasonings. Cover the bowl at once and keep covered a few minutes until the butter and blue cheese have melted. Stir and correct the seasoning.

Serves 2

Baked Eggplant

This recipe eliminates a good deal of work and fat because it omits the sautéing step, in which the eggplant soaks up great quantities of oil. Steaming the eggplant dispenses with the usual preliminaries of salting and draining needed to get rid of the natural bitterness. You may, if you wish, substitute 1 cup of milk for the second can of tomato sauce. The mixture produces a pleasant flavor that is somewhat less sharp than that of tomato sauce alone. Good served over cooked, drained pasta (cavatelli, rigatoni, shells, etc.).

1 large eggplant
2 8-ounce cans tomato
  sauce
4 ounces provolone or
  mozzarella cheese, diced

¼ teaspoon garlic powder
¼ teaspoon dried oregano
¼ teaspoon dried basil
salt and pepper to taste

Preheat the oven to 325°.

1 Wash and slice the eggplant in ½-inch slices. Do not peel.

2 Place the slices in a vegetable steamer, cover, and steam 8 to 10 minutes. Remove the slices carefully with a slotted pancake turner and arrange half of them in a greased oven-proof dish.

3 Pour 1 can of tomato sauce over the layer of eggplant and sprinkle with half the seasonings as evenly as you can. Dot with half the cheese. Repeat the process, making a second layer of eggplant, tomato sauce, seasonings, and cheese. Bake for 30 minutes uncovered.

Serves 4

"Crispy and Delicious" Green Beans

Green beans prepared in this way can often be found in Chinese restaurants, though you may want to dispense with the bits of shaved cooked pork. Be sure not to overcook the beans: 5 minutes in a covered pan should be enough.

¾ pound green beans
2 tablespoons peanut, safflower, corn, or olive oil
½ cup cooked pork, cut
  in tiny shreds

3 *cloves garlic, peeled*
salt to taste

1 Cut off the ends of the green beans. Wash but do not dry them.

2 Mash the garlic* and heat the oil in a skillet over medium-high heat. Add the garlic to the oil for about 1 minute.

3 Add the wet green beans to the hot oil and garlic and cover immediately. Shake the pan, uncovering occasionally to stir well. Cook 3 to 5 minutes, depending on how cooked you like them. When they are almost done, add the cooked pork, stir well, and cover until just heated through. Add salt before serving.

Serves 3

  * See page 19 for mashing garlic cloves.

Leeks Rissolés

This is a simple French family dish. The flavor of the leeks takes on an added dimension as the leeks acquire a golden crust.

2 whole leeks
flour for dredging
2 tablespoons safflower,
   corn, or olive oil

salt and pepper to taste

1 Cut off the roots of the leeks and remove the outer blades as well as any that are damaged or withered. Before washing, slit the green ends vertically, making two 2-inch cuts so that tap water can flush away any hidden dirt. Cut the leeks in half, crosswise.

2 Steam or parboil about 15 minutes. Drain. Dredge them with flour.

3 Heat the oil over medium heat. Place the leeks carefully in the oil. Turn when they are golden brown or "rissolés" and cook on the other side. Season.

Serves 2 generously

Marinated Leeks

This is a good recipe to apply to Brussels sprouts, green beans, zucchini, cauliflower, and green or red peppers. (See page 121 for cooking times.) Vegetables prepared in this way make an excellent first course.

4 whole leeks
½ cup olive oil
3 tablespoons wine
  vinegar

1 tablespoon Dijon
  mustard
1 tablespoon chopped
  parsley
1 clove garlic, peeled and
  minced
salt and pepper to taste

Optional:
sliced Calamata olives,
  capers, minced scallion

1 Wash the leeks well (see page 132) and cut them into 3-inch lengths.

2 Steam them by the method given on page 121 about 15 minutes. Remove them from the heat, drain, and place them in a bowl.

3 Mix together the oil, vinegar, and seasonings. Add the olives, capers, and scallions, if you wish. Pour the marinade over the leeks and marinate for 2 hours, turning them from time to time.

Serves 4

Baked Onions

This is an easily made dish that is very compatible with roast chicken or pork—a good combination that can be cooked in the same oven.

4 large onions
2 ounces Swiss cheese
¾ cup light cream or milk

salt and pepper to taste

Optional:
4 tablespoons dry sherry

Preheat the oven to 350°.

1 Peel and slice the onions and place them in a greased ovenproof dish.

2 Grate or dice the Swiss cheese; mix with the cream or milk (and, if you wish, the sherry). Pour over the onions. Season.

3 Bake for 30 minutes.

Serves 4

Parsnip Puree

Parsnips prepared in this way are delectable. Parsnips often come waxed; waxing preserves them but also makes paring rather difficult. One solution is to put waxed vegetables in the freezer for a short time, then give them a sharp smack against the side of the sink. The wax will usually fragment and fall off.

4 medium-sized parsnips
½ cup milk or light cream
2 tablespoons butter

½ teaspoon salt
pinch of freshly grated
   nutmeg
pepper to taste

1 Pare the parsnips and cut them into 1-inch slices. Cover them with water and boil 10 minutes.

2 Pour the milk or cream into the blender. Drain the cooked parsnips and place them in the blender, along with the butter and seasonings.

3 Blend well for a few seconds, correct the seasoning, and serve.

Serves 2

Roasted Peppers

These very delicious peppers need some advance planning. If you broil them a few hours before serving, they will have a chance to cool (and you won't risk burning your fingers peeling them), and the longer they marinate, the better they will be.

2 large green peppers
2 large red peppers
2 tablespoons olive oil

1 clove garlic, peeled and
*   minced*
salt and pepper to taste

Preheat the broiler.

1 Wash the peppers and place them in a pan under the broiler, turning them to allow the skin to blister and char on all sides. Remove the peppers from the broiler and place them in a paper bag to cool.

2 When the peppers are cool enough to handle, peel them and cut them into slices, removing the seeds.

3 Arrange the slices on a serving dish, alternating red and green slices. Cover with the olive oil and seasonings, and marinate for at least 30 minutes before serving.

Note: You may wish to add Calamata olives or capers, a few chopped anchovies, or a tablespoon or two of seasoned Italian bread crumbs: any are standard variations for this version of Italian roasted peppers.

Serves 2

Mashed Potatoes

Mashed potatoes can be dreary or perfectly wonderful, depending on the care with which they are cooked. If you leave the potatoes unpeeled, the whole procedure takes no longer than 15 minutes.

2 medium or large boiling
  potatoes
3 tablespoons butter
⅓ cup milk or light cream

salt and pepper to taste

1 Peel the potatoes or leave them unpeeled (in which case scrub them well), as you prefer. Cut into pieces or slices and drop into a saucepan of boiling salted water to cover. Meanwhile, in a small saucepan heat the milk or cream over low heat, being careful not to let it boil.

2 When the potatoes are soft but not disintegrating, drain in a colander and return to the saucepan. Shake the pan vigorously over low heat for a minute or two so that the potatoes give up any excess moisture. Drying them out—without letting them burn—avoids watery mashed potatoes.

3 Mash the potatoes with a potato ricer or masher, add the butter, and mix well. When the butter has melted, add the heated milk or cream and mix well again. Add the seasonings.

Variations: Add 1 clove of garlic during boiling, being sure to remove it before mashing the potatoes.
  Or, at the very end, add one of the following:
    ¼ teaspoon freshly grated nutmeg
    1 tablespoon finely minced fresh parsley
    2 tablespoons grated Parmesan, Swiss, or Cheddar
      cheese
    1 heaping tablespoon sour cream and 1 tablespoon
      chopped fresh chives

Serves 2

Boiled New Potatoes

New potatoes are one of the pleasures of spring-in-the-super-market. Look for pale brown potatoes rather than those that have been dyed red; if you have no choice, then be sure to peel them before boiling.

4 cups water	1 teaspoon salt
1 pound small new potatoes	salt and pepper to taste
3 tablespoons butter	2 tablespoons chopped watercress or parsley

1 Heat the water in a pot and add 1 teaspoon of salt. Meanwhile, wash the potatoes well, scrubbing gently with a vegetable brush. When the water comes to a good boil, place the potatoes in the pot. Let the water return to a boil and then reduce the heat. Let the potatoes cook 12 to 15 minutes, partly covered, or until tender when pierced with a sharp knife.

2 Drain the potatoes in a colander and put them back in the pot. Cook over very low heat 1 to 2 minutes, shaking the pan to dry the potatoes out.

3 Add the butter and let it melt, turning the potatoes a few times to coat them with the butter. Season with salt and pepper. Sprinkle with watercress or parsley.

Serves 2 generously

French-Fried Sweet Potatoes

This distinguished recipe was given to me by Mr. Stanley Demos, owner of the Coach House Restaurant in Lexington, Kentucky. The recipe calls for precooking (Step 2), then completing the frying (Step 3) just before serving. To prepare this accurately, you should have a candy thermometer. These potatoes go wonderfully with ham or poultry.

2 large sweet potatoes
enough vegetable oil for
  deep frying

1 teaspoon ground cinna-
  mon
1 teaspoon sugar

1 Peel the sweet potatoes and cut them so that they resemble french-fried potatoes. Wash and blot dry with paper or cloth towels.

2 Slowly heat the oil in a deep pot until it reaches 200° on a candy thermometer. Carefully drop in a few slices at a time and fry until they are just cooked but not brown. (They should be easily pierced by a fork.) Remove from the oil with a slotted spoon and spread them on paper towels to drain.

3 Just before serving, deep-fry them in 350° oil until golden brown.* Watch carefully and do not allow them to brown too much. Remove and drain on fresh paper towels. Mix the sugar and cinnamon and sprinkle generously over the potatoes. Serve at once.

Serves 4

* You will need to raise the heat after dropping the potatoes in the oil in order to maintain the 350° temperature.

Potato Pancake Crust

This is an unusual pie crust. It contains no fat and can be filled with a layer of cooked vegetables (sautéed and drained) and a layer of cottage cheese, then baked further until the cheese melts. Or this crust can be filled with applesauce and/or sour cream, traditional accompaniments to potato pancakes. Either way, here is a good solution to a meatless dinner.

2 medium-sized boiling
  potatoes
1 small onion
1 egg

1 teaspoon dried parsley
½–¾ teaspoon salt
pepper to taste

Preheat the oven to 350°.

1 Grate the potatoes in a food processor or by hand using a coarse grater and place them in a colander over a bowl. Press out as much water as you can. Discard the liquid collected in the bowl.

2 Peel and grate the onion. Beat the egg in the bowl and add the grated potatoes, onion, and seasonings. Mix well.

3 Line a greased 9-inch pie plate with the mixture. Bake 25 to 30 minutes, or until brown.

Note: If you are filling the crust with vegetables and cheese, add them to the shell after 20 minutes and reduce the heat to 250°. Return to the oven for 10 minutes, or just until the cheese melts.

Makes a 9-inch crust

Broiled Potatoes

For people who must avoid the large amount of oil needed for french-frying—or who hate the trouble and mess—these potatoes are every bit as good.

2 large baking potatoes
3 tablespoons safflower or
   corn oil

salt and pepper to taste

Preheat the broiler.

1 Scrub the potatoes, dry them thoroughly with paper towels, and slice as thinly as possible.

2 Spread the oil evenly over a large broiling pan. Arrange the potato slices so that they don't overlap. Turn to coat them with oil and season well.

3 Place in the broiler, about 5 inches from the heat. When the potatoes brown on one side, turn them and brown on the other. They are ready when they brown and puff up slightly. Watch closely so that they don't burn.

Serves 2 generously

Sautéed Red Radishes

This unusual way of preparing radishes produces a cooked vegetable that is interesting in its own right and can also serve as a garnish for other vegetables or rice. You may want to try cooking other varieties of radishes in this way.

2 bunches large red radishes
1 tablespoon peanut, safflower, or corn oil
1 tablespoon butter or margarine

salt and pepper to taste

1 Wash the radishes and dry them with paper towels. Slice the radishes thinly.

2 Heat the oil and butter in a skillet, add the sliced radishes and cook a few minutes on each side.

3 Season and serve.

Serves 2

Fried Green Tomatoes

The tartness of green tomatoes is considerably tamed by frying. Prepared in this way, they make a pleasant and invigorating cooked vegetable.

2 or 3 large green
  tomatoes
½ cup herbed bread
  crumbs
3 tablespoons peanut,
  safflower, or corn oil

salt and pepper to taste

Optional:
1 egg, beaten

1 Wash and dry the tomatoes. Cut them into ¼-inch slices and season them with salt and pepper.

2 Spread the bread crumbs out on a large plate. Arrange the tomato slices over the bread crumbs, pushing them gently into the crumbs and turning to coat well. (You may, if you wish, dip each slice in beaten egg before coating with the bread crumbs.)

3 Heat the oil in an enameled or stainless-steel skillet over medium heat and fry the tomato slices, turning each slice until brown—about 3 minutes on each side.

Serves 2 generously

Grated Sautéed Zucchini

In this recipe, as in the recipes for glazed carrots and grated cabbage, grating speeds up the cooking time and is a welcome change from the usual ways of cooking vegetables.

4–6 small zucchini
2 scallions
2 tablespoons olive oil
    or butter

¼ teaspoon dried dillweed
2 tablespoons chopped
    fresh parsley
salt and pepper to taste

1 Scrub but do not peel the zucchini. Grate in the food processor or with a hand grater, using the coarse side. Place the grated zucchini in a colander for 10 minutes and let it drain, pressing the liquid out from time to time with a spoon.

2 Chop the scallions. Heat the oil or butter in a skillet, add the scallions, and sauté them. The moment they become translucent, add the grated zucchini and the dill.

3 Stir-fry for 2 to 3 minutes, cooking over medium-high heat. Cover for 1 to 2 minutes. Add the parsley, salt, and pepper just before serving and mix well.

Serves 2

FOUR-INGREDIENT RECIPES

Cauliflower Puree
with Cheese

This recipe makes cauliflower more interesting than it is generally thought to be. Just avoid the mistake of the cook who served boiled cauliflower with boiled fish and mashed potatoes—a very white meal—by serving this recipe with ham and green noodles.

1 small head cauliflower
4 tablespoons grated
   Swiss cheese
2 tablespoons butter
¼ cup light or heavy
   cream or milk

salt and pepper to taste

Preheat the oven to 350°.

1 Remove the green stalks and leaves from the cauliflower. Cut off the tough ends of the white stalks and separate the florets. Steam the cauliflower about 12 minutes, or until it is soft. Puree it in the blender for 6 to 8 seconds at high speed. Season with salt and pepper.

2 Pour half the puree in a greased pie plate. Sprinkle 2 tablespoons of cheese over the puree and 1 tablespoon of butter. Add the remaining puree and the remaining cheese and butter.

3 Pour the cream or milk over the puree and bake it for 15 minutes, or until the surface is golden.

Serves 4

Falafel Cake

This recipe vastly simplifies the making of falafel—no need to shape into little balls, and no need to deep-fry. Prepared this way, falafel becomes a relatively low-fat, low-cholesterol recipe. It's just as good the second night, either reheated or served at room temperature.

2 eggs
2 cups cooked or canned chick-peas, drained
1 small onion, peeled and sliced
2 tablespoons safflower or corn oil

1 clove garlic, peeled
small handful fresh parsley
¼ teaspoon each turmeric, mace, and powdered cumin
1 teaspoon salt
pepper to taste

Preheat the oven to 350°.

1 Place the eggs, chick-peas, onion, and seasonings in a food processor or blender. Process or blend, but not too finely (the batter should be fairly grainy—not a puree).

2 Heat the oil in a 10½-inch cast-iron skillet on medium heat. Pour in the batter and cook for 10 minutes.

3 Place in the oven and bake 15 to 20 minutes, or until crusty.

Note: Excellent served garnished with yogurt, chopped tomatoes and cucumbers, and if you like, chopped onions or scallions.

Serves 4

Baked Fennel or Finocchio

This vegetable can often be found in supermarkets, particularly in Italian neighborhoods. Eaten raw it is an excellent hors d'oeuvre, much like the best celery in texture, with a distinctive aromatic flavor similar to that of licorice. In Italy, mixed salad often contains slices of fresh fennel. This recipe goes very well with chicken or roast pork or lamb.

1 medium fennel
2 teaspoons butter
2 teaspoons light cream
2 teaspoons grated Parmesan cheese

Preheat the oven to 300°.

1 Cut off the base and the green tendrils.* Wash and cut the fennel in half lengthwise.

2 Boil 10 to 15 minutes. Drain.

3 Arrange on a small oiled baking dish. Place 1 teaspoon butter, 1 teaspoon cream, and 1 teaspoon Parmesan cheese over each half and bake for 10 minutes.

Serves 2

* Save the green tendrils to flavor steamed rice or fish. Place the tendrils over the rice, then cover and steam; or place them over the fish, using aluminum foil or parchment paper to wrap the fish and the fennel, and steam. Discard the tendrils before serving.

Mushrooms on Toast

This open-faced sandwich, a traditional English dish, makes a perfect lunch anywhere. Allow 2 per person. These mushrooms can, of course, serve as a vegetable on their own without toast.

½ pound mushrooms
2 tablespoons butter
½ cup light cream or milk
4 slices white bread, toasted

pinch freshly grated nutmeg
salt and pepper to taste

1 Wipe or wash the mushrooms.* Slice the mushrooms vertically without removing the stems.

2 Heat the butter over medium-high heat, and when hot, sauté the mushrooms 3 to 5 minutes, stirring occasionally.

3 Pour on the cream or milk, lower the heat, and simmer uncovered until the liquid has been absorbed. Season and serve on freshly made toast.

Serves 2

* There are two schools of thought about cleaning mushrooms. Some cooks prefer just to wipe them with a damp cloth. Others want to *wash* them clean. In either case, there is no need to peel them.

Onion Tart

This tart needs no further baking, as long as you have a baked pie crust ready. If you wish, however, you may arrange the ingredients in an unbaked shell and bake 15 minutes at 400°. Either way, the success of this simple dish depends largely on the quality of the onions and tomatoes. The sweeter the onions and the riper the tomatoes, the better the tart. Use Spanish onions if you can and homegrown rather than supermarket tomatoes.

1 prebaked pie crust,
  preferably homemade
4 large onions
¼ cup olive oil
3 ripe tomatoes

½ teaspoon dried thyme,
  divided
½ teaspoon dried basil,
  divided
salt and pepper to taste

Optional:
several Greek or Calamata
  olives, sliced and pitted
several anchovies

1 Peel and dice the onions. Heat the oil in a skillet, add the onions, and sauté them over low heat until almost brown. Stir from time to time. Season with ¼ teaspoon thyme, ¼ teaspoon basil, and salt and pepper. (Be careful not to over-salt if you plan to use anchovies at the end.)

2 Fill the pie shell with the mixture.

3 Slice the tomatoes and arrange them over the onions. Sprinkle with the remaining thyme and basil and a few drops of olive oil. Add salt and pepper carefully. Garnish, if you wish, with olives and anchovies.

Serves 6

Green Peas in the Lebanese Manner, or Bezela

This is a vegetarian adaptation by a Lebanese friend of a dish that usually includes meat. As a variation, you may want to include crumbled feta cheese or bean curd—as much or as little as you like.

With or without variations, this dish is good served around a mound of cooked brown rice seasoned with cinnamon.

2 medium onions
1–2 tablespoons olive oil
2 fresh tomatoes
10-ounce package frozen
   peas

¼ teaspoon allspice
¼ teaspoon garlic powder
salt and pepper to taste

1 Chop the onions. Heat the oil in a skillet over medium-high heat. Add the onions and sauté until they begin to brown, 10 to 12 minutes.

2 Chop the tomatoes and add, juice and all, to the onions.

3 Add the peas and the seasonings. Cook until peas are thawed and heated through, about 8 to 10 minutes. Do not overcook. Mix well and correct seasoning.

Serves 2 generously

Simmered Peppers

Use red peppers or green peppers or both. You may wish to sauté the onions first and then add the other ingredients; whatever method you use, the long simmering produces an excellent flavor.

1 onion
4 medium to large red
  and/or green peppers
3 fresh tomatoes
2 tablespoons olive oil

¼ teaspoon dried oregano
salt and pepper to taste

1 Slice the onion, peppers, and tomatoes in a food processor. If you slice by hand, be sure to slice thinly.

2 Place all the vegetables in a saucepan with the olive oil.

3 Bring carefully to a boil and simmer 40 to 60 minutes, covered. You may wish to remove the cover the last 10 minutes of cooking to let some of the liquid in the saucepan evaporate, but be careful not to let the peppers burn.

Serves 4

Simple Potato Soufflé

Any time you are planning to bake potatoes, double the number so that you can prepare this very good dish the following evening.

2 large baked potatoes
2 eggs
1 small onion
2 tablespoons melted butter or safflower or corn oil

salt and pepper to taste

Preheat the oven to 350°.

1 Scoop out the baked potatoes and mash. Beat the eggs.

2 Grate the onion or chop it finely. Mix with the potato and eggs, add the butter, and season.

3 Bake in an oiled pan 15 to 20 minutes, or until the surface of the potatoes begins to brown.

Serves 2 generously

Pumpkin Pudding

This pudding supplies all the comfort and reassurance of pumpkin pie without the calories contributed by the crust. Serve either as a dessert or as a vegetable to accompany turkey, chicken, or pork.

3 eggs
16-ounce can pumpkin
¾ cup loosely packed light brown sugar*
1½ cups milk or light cream (or 13-ounce can evaporated milk)

1 teaspoon ground cinnamon
1 teaspoon powdered cardamom
½ teaspoon freshly grated ginger
¼ teaspoon ground cloves
pinch of salt

Preheat the oven to 350°.

1 Beat the eggs.

2 Add all the other ingredients and mix together, beating with a hand beater or using a food processor or blender. Place the mixture in an oiled 8- or 9-inch round baking dish.†

3 Bake 45 minutes or until a knife inserted in the center comes out clean.

Serves 6 to 8

* If you serve this as a vegetable, you may want to reduce the amount of sugar to ½ cup.
† If you serve this as a dessert, try baking it in oiled custard cups. You will need 7 or 8, depending on how high you fill them.

Spinach Bhurta

This adaptation of a spinach recipe from India can be used as a condiment as well as a vegetable. If you have the time, by all means use fresh spinach (allow 1 pound for 2 people) and wash it well in cold water, changing the water a few times until no sand is left.

10-ounce package frozen
  chopped spinach
2 onions
2 tablespoons butter
½ cup yogurt, sour cream,
  or cottage cheese

*cayenne pepper to taste**
salt to taste

Optional:
¼ *teaspoon powdered*
  cumin

1 Cook the spinach according to the directions on the package. Place the spinach in a colander and press out as much water as you can.

2 Chop the onions. In an enameled skillet, heat the butter over medium heat, and when it is hot, add the onions and sauté them 8 to 10 minutes until golden.

3 Add all the other ingredients to the onions. Mix well and heat through, stirring for 5 minutes (or with cottage cheese, until it melts). Taste and correct the seasoning. If you use a good deal of cayenne, you may want to add a little more yogurt, sour cream, or cottage cheese. Mix well and heat a few minutes longer.

Serves 2 generously

* If you're unfamiliar with cayenne, start with a pinch, mix, and taste before adding a little more.

SALADS

Apple and Beet Salad

An interesting combination of flavors—very good with pork or chicken.

1 medium-sized tart apple	¼ teaspoon dried dillweed
3–4 fresh beets	¼ teaspoon celery seed
2 tablespoons mayonnaise, preferably homemade (page 174)	salt to taste

1 Peel and chop the apple.

2 Wash and peel the beets. Cook according to the directions on page 123.

3 Dice the cooked beets and mix with the apples, mayonnaise, and seasonings. Chill for several hours before serving.

Serves 2

White Bean Salad

This standard Italian appetizer makes a fine main course on a hot day. You may use canned white beans or start from scratch with dried ones following the package directions (or see page 278).

3 tablespoons olive oil
1 tablespoon wine vinegar
15-ounce can white beans
    (Great Northern beans),
    drained and rinsed, or
    1½ cups cooked white
    beans (page 278)

½ teaspoon Dijon mustard
salt and pepper to taste

Optional:
slivers of ham, salami,
    Greek olives, tomato,
    onion, chopped raw
    spinach leaves

1 Combine the oil and vinegar with the mustard.

2 Add to the beans (with any of the optional ingredients you wish).

3 Toss to combine, season to taste, and serve at room temperature.

Serves 2

Carrot Salad

This classic health food salad is guaranteed to keep up your strength.

6 carrots
½–¾ cup unflavored
    yogurt
2–3 tablespoons honey

¼ teaspoon ground
    cinnamon
pinch of salt

1 Pare the carrots and grate in a processor or on a grater, using the coarse side.

2 Add the yogurt, honey, cinnamon, and salt.

3 Mix well and chill before serving.

Serves 2 generously

Cucumber Salad

If you follow this procedure—not much trouble, really—the cucumbers will have a very good texture.

2 cucumbers
½ cup sour cream or
  yogurt
several pecans or walnuts

⅛ teaspoon powdered
  cumin
salt and pepper to taste

Optional:
1 scallion, finely minced

1 Two hours before serving time, peel the cucumbers and slice them as thinly as possible (if you can see the knife through the last slice, you're cutting thinly enough). Salt the cucumbers generously and place them in a bowl. Cover and refrigerate.

2 At serving time, press a heavy plate down on the cucumbers and invert the bowl, holding the plate in place. Drain well to remove as much liquid as you can. The salt will have drawn out the water from the cucumbers, so that they should be very crisp.

3 Mix lightly with the sour cream or yogurt, the nuts, and seasonings. Garnish with the minced scallions, if you wish.

Serves 2

Grape and Watercress Salad

This is a superb salad, just the thing for special occasions. Try to allow enough time so that the watercress can crisp in the ice water before you make the salad.

½ pound green seedless
   grapes
1 small bunch watercress
2 tablespoons mayon-
   naise, preferably homemade (page 174)

Optional:
2 *tablespoons light or*
   heavy cream

1 Wash and cut the grapes in half.

2 Wash the watercress, cutting off any tough or discolored ends. Soak in ice water 20 minutes. Shake dry. Cut off the stems and save for use in other salads or soups or stews.

3 Place the grapes and the watercress in alternate layers in a glass bowl and garnish with mayonnaise or, if you wish, a mixture of mayonnaise and cream. Toss at the table.

Serves 2

Egg Salad

This egg salad is made with sour cream rather than mayonnaise.

4 eggs
2 heaping tablespoons sour cream
1 tablespoon olive oil

1 teaspoon Dijon mustard
salt and pepper to taste

Optional:
1 teaspoon capers

1 Cook the eggs following the rule for hard-cooked eggs (see page 276).

2 Peel and mash the eggs with a fork or in a food processor—the smoother the texture, the better.

3 Add the sour cream, oil, and seasonings and mix well. Garnish with capers, if you wish; or, for a contrast in texture, mix them into the salad (but only *after* it has been mashed or processed).

Serves 2

Corned Beef and Pickle Salad

The success of this salad depends largely on the quality of the mayonnaise. It's worth the trouble to prepare your own mayonnaise. Once that's done, you'll have an excellent lunch dish for guests. Serve with rye toast.

½ **pound corned beef**
6–8 **miniature sweet gherkins**
¼ **cup mayonnaise (preferably homemade, page 174)**

1 Trim the fat and dice the corned beef.

2 Drain and chop the pickles.

3 Combine and mix well with mayonnaise.

Note: If you are pressed for time, you can use a good-quality commercial mayonnaise and add enough lemon juice to it for a tarter taste and looser consistency.

Serves 2

Ham and Melon Salad

Prosciutto and melon are a standard first course in Italy. This version makes a salad of it, very suitable as the main course for a light lunch for guests. Fresh figs are an excellent substitute for melon.

½ pound prosciutto or boiled or baked ham, sliced thin
1 small cantaloupe, musk melon, or honeydew, or
    4 fresh figs
3 tablespoons mayonnaise (preferably homemade,
    page 174)

1 Trim as much fat as you can from the prosciutto or ham and cut it into small pieces.

2 Slice the melon into eighths, then peel and scrape away the seeds from each section and cut into thin slices.

3 Combine the ham and melon and mix with the mayonnaise. Chill for several hours.

Serves 2 generously

Chick-Pea Salad

This recipe takes no more time than a peanut butter and jelly sandwich and will provide a welcome change at lunch time.

15-ounce can chick-peas or 1½ cups cooked chick-peas (page 278)
2 tablespoons olive oil
½ lemon

small handful fresh parsley, minced
½ teaspoon dried mint
pinch of garlic powder
salt and pepper to taste
½ teaspoon toasted sesame seeds

1 Drain the chick-peas and place in a bowl.

2 Toss with olive oil.

3 Squeeze the lemon and add the juice and seasonings to the chick-peas. Toss. Sprinkle sesame seeds over the salad just before serving.

Serves 2

Roman Potato Salad

This potato salad is far less likely to spoil than the more familiar kind made with mayonnaise. For this reason the following recipe is especially good for picnics and buffet parties.

3 large boiling potatoes
⅛ cup olive oil
1 scallion, finely chopped

salt and pepper to taste

1 Scrub the potatoes and cut them in half lengthwise, leaving the skins on. Place in boiling water and boil for 10 minutes, or until a fork can easily pierce them. Do not overcook.

2 When the potatoes are cool enough to handle, peel them if you wish (they're more nutritious unpeeled) and dice them.

3 While they're still warm, toss them with the olive oil and scallion. Season to taste and serve at room temperature.

Serves 4

FOUR-INGREDIENT RECIPES

Carrot and Turnip Salad

If you've never had grated raw turnips, this is a good way to try them. The contrast in colors makes a nice effect.

1 small turnip
4 carrots
½ cup yogurt
2 tablespoons honey

salt to taste

Optional
*(any of the following):
raisins, chopped dried
apricots, slivered apple,
nuts (pecans, walnuts,
hazelnuts, cashews, pea-
nuts, soybean nuts)*

1 Peel and grate the turnip and carrots in a food processor or on the coarse side of a food grater.

2 Add the yogurt and honey to the grated vegetables and mix well. Season. (If desired, add any of the suggested fruits or nuts.)

3 Chill for several hours before serving.

Serves 2

Coleslaw

Although this can be prepared without the carrots and green pepper, the differing textures and colors add a pleasant touch.

½ small head cabbage
2 medium-sized carrots
1 medium-sized green
   pepper
Dressing for Coleslaw
   (page 175)

Optional:
1 large apple, peeled,
   cored, and chopped

1 Remove and discard the outer leaves of the cabbage. Shred the cabbage in a food processor or grate finely by hand.

2 Pare and wash the carrots. Grate them.

3 Wash and seed the pepper. Cut it into thin slivers. Place all the vegetables (and the apple, if you wish) in a bowl large enough for mixing. Cover and chill for at least 3 hours. Add the dressing just before serving.

Serves 4

Chicken or Ham Salad

In this recipe, fresh fruit revitalizes leftover meat. Feel free to substitute turkey, pork, or veal, combining any or all.

2 **cups diced cooked chicken or ham**
2 **stalks celery**
1–2 **cups apples, canta-loupe, pears, oranges, pineapple, kiwi, or seedless grapes**
3 **tablespoons mayonnaise (preferably homemade, page 174)**

few leaves fresh mint, chopped, or ¼ teaspoon dried mint
salt to taste

1 Dice the celery.

2 Peel the fruit and dice it. (If you are using grapes, wash them and either leave them whole or cut them in half, as you prefer.)

3 Mix all the ingredients, including the seasonings, in a large bowl. Chill for several hours before serving.

Serves 2 generously

Meat Salad, or Fleischsalat

This salad, popular in Germany and Austria, deserves to be better known here. It's good for summer lunches or dinners and an excellent dish for buffet suppers.

1 small sweet onion
1 tomato
2 cups diced leftover roast beef or veal
3 tablespoons mayonnaise (preferably homemade, page 174)

¼ teaspoon Dijon mustard
salt and pepper to taste

Optional:
½ cup diced cooked vegetables (beets, carrots, potatoes, or peas), or
½ cup diced raw vegetables (cucumbers, celery, or green pepper)

1 Chop the onion.

2 Chop the tomato.

3 Combine the meat, onion, and tomato with mayonnaise. Add the seasonings and mix. Chill for several hours before serving.

Serves 2

Smoked Fish Salad

This wonderful salad goes very well with sliced tomatoes and ripe olives.

1 egg
¼ pound smoked whitefish
1 avocado
1–2 tablespoons olive oil

Optional:
few drops lemon juice

1 Hard-cook the egg according to the instructions on page 276. Peel and mash with a fork.

2 Bone and flake the fish. Peel and slice the avocado.

3 Combine all the ingredients with the oil. Sprinkle with lemon juice, if you like.

Serves 2

Bulgur Wheat Salad, or Tabouli

This refreshing and substantial salad is best prepared in summer, when tomatoes are at their peak and fresh mint is available. The conventional method of preparing bulgur wheat for tabouli is simply to cover it with cold water, let it soak for 20 minutes, and then drain it. But the flavor of the salad seems to me much improved if the bulgur is first prepared by the rule for cooking (see page 68), in which case the kernels acquire a roasted flavor before they soak up the liquid. (Just be sure to let the bulgur cool before proceeding with the salad.)

1 scallion
2 tomatoes
2 cups cooked bulgur wheat
3 tablespoons olive oil

1 bunch parsley, finely chopped
few leaves fresh mint, finely chopped, or ½ teaspoon dried mint leaves
salt and pepper to taste

Optional:
lemon juice to taste

1 Chop the scallion and tomatoes.

2 Mix with the cooled bulgur.

3 Dress with the olive oil. Add the seasonings and mix well. Serve at room temperature.

Serves 2 generously

Pasta Salad

This is such a good way to use leftover pasta that you may want to cook twice the amount you need for one meal in order to have enough for the next day's pasta salad. The salad lends itself to so much variation you'll probably never fix it the same way twice. A good variety of vegetables adds color as well as flavor and contrasts in texture.

¼ pound cooked pasta
(macaroni, tubes, or
shells)
3–4 tablespoons olive oil
1 tomato, chopped
1–2 cups chopped fresh
vegetables (any one or
a combination of onion,
celery, green pepper,
red pepper, cucumber)

½ teaspoon dried basil
½ teaspoon dried thyme
pinch of garlic powder
salt and pepper to taste

Optional:
several green and/or black
olives, slivered
1–2 teaspoons capers

1 Cook the pasta according to the directions on the package. When the pasta is done, drain and toss with oil.

2 Add the tomato, vegetables, and seasonings.

3 Mix well, and serve at room temperature.

Serves 2

SALAD DRESSINGS, SAUCES, & CONDIMENTS

Basic Salad Dressing for Green Salad

6 tablespoons olive oil
2 tablespoons wine vinegar
or lemon juice

salt and pepper to taste

1 Combine the oil and vinegar in a jar with a tight-fitting lid.

2 Shake well until the oil and vinegar are thoroughly blended.

3 Add the seasonings and shake again.

Variations: Add 1 tablespoon grated Parmesan cheese or
2 tablespoons crumbled blue cheese or
½ teaspoon Dijon mustard
or
1 tablespoon sour cream
any of the following dried herbs:
¼ teaspoon basil, ¼ teaspoon dillweed,
¼ teaspoon tarragon or chervil,
¼ teaspoon chives, ¼ teaspoon oregano

Note: You may wish to combine some of these variations. With any of them, you may wish to rub the bowl with a cut clove of garlic. In any case, use the best olive oil you can and always prepare the dressing freshly for each use.
Makes ½ cup

Blender Mayonnaise

One of the great boons to mankind, the blender makes short work of what was once a laborious process, undertaken only by the most devoted—to real mayonnaise.

1 egg
2 tablespoons wine vinegar
　or lemon juice
1 cup safflower, corn, or
　olive oil,* divided

½ teaspoon mustard
　powder
¼ teaspoon salt

1 Place the egg, vinegar, and seasonings in the blender with ¼ cup of the oil.

2 Cover and blend on *low speed* for a few seconds until smooth.

3 Do not turn the blender off, but uncover carefully and *slowly* pour the remaining oil into the center of the mixture. Blend until homogenized and as thick as recognizable mayonnaise. Correct the seasoning and blend for another second.

Variations:
Aioli is a garlic mayonnaise that is a standard accompaniment in the south of France to vegetables, fish, boiled meat, and boiled chicken. To make it, add 2 cloves of peeled garlic to the egg and proceed as you would in making plain mayonnaise.

For *green mayonnaise*, add a few fresh spinach leaves, a few sprigs of watercress and/or parsley, ¼ teaspoon tarragon or chervil. Adjust the seasoning (you will probably need more than ¼ teaspoon salt).

For a very good *fruit salad dressing*, add an equal amount of whipped cream to completed safflower or corn oil mayonnaise (or use any proportions you prefer). Stir well.

For *blue cheese dressing*, add 3 tablespoons crumbled blue cheese and 3 tablespoons heavy cream to the completed mayonnaise. Stir well.

Makes about 1 cup

* To make mayonnaise for use in fruit dishes, stick to safflower or corn oil rather than olive oil, which has too pronounced a flavor and one that is not compatible with fruit.

Dressing for Coleslaw or Shredded Carrot Salad

This is simply the best coleslaw dressing I know of. I was introduced to it by a friend from Kansas, where the recipe appears to have originated. If this dressing strikes you as too rich, substitute milk or buttermilk.

2–3 tablespoons sugar
½ cup heavy or light
  cream
2½ tablespoons cider
  vinegar

½ *teaspoon salt*

1 Combine the ingredients in the order given.

2 Refrigerate covered for 2 to 3 hours.

3 At serving time, combine with chilled shredded vegetables in a chilled bowl and toss to mix well.

Makes about ¾ cup

Anchovy Sauce, or Bagna Cauda

This is what Americans would call a hot dip; Italians call it a hot bath. While it was intended for raw vegetables, it is also good with cooked vegetables, pasta, hard-cooked eggs, and, of course, Italian bread sticks.

½ cup olive oil or butter
8 anchovies, minced
½ cup light cream

2 *large cloves garlic, peeled and minced*

1 Heat the oil or butter and garlic, being careful not to allow the garlic to burn.

2 Add the anchovies and mix.

3 Add the cream, mix, and heat over low heat. Do not allow to boil.

Note: Used as a dip, this sauce should be kept warm in a small chafing dish.

Makes about 1 cup

Onion Sauce, or Puree Soubise

This excellent accompaniment to roast lamb or veal is also a very useful way of reheating—and refurbishing—leftovers from the roast. After you blend the sauce, return it to the saucepan and place over it as many slices of cooked meat as you wish. Cover the saucepan and heat through on low heat.

3 large onions
½ cup milk
1–2 tablespoons butter

¼ teaspoon freshly grated nutmeg
1 teaspoon salt
pepper to taste

Optional:
1 ounce Swiss cheese

1 Peel the onions, slice them, and place them in a small saucepan.

2 Cover the onions with the milk, cover the pan, and bring to a boil. Reduce the heat and cook 10 to 15 minutes, or until the onions are soft. Add the butter and seasonings (and the cheese, if you like). Cook 2 to 3 more minutes.

3 Pour the contents of the saucepan into the blender jar. Process at high speed until the sauce is smooth, about 6 to 7 minutes.

Makes enough sauce for 3 to 4 portions of meat

Green Sauce,
or Salsa Verde

This is the standard Italian sauce that accompanies boiled meat or sometimes fish. Use it also with plain steamed vegetables like broccoli, leeks, green beans, or spinach to give them a special character. (If you use it on spinach or with spinach salad, omit the optional spinach leaves.)

½ small onion
3 tablespoons olive oil
3 tablespoons wine vinegar

1 teaspoon capers,
  chopped
1 clove garlic, peeled and
  minced
3 tablespoons chopped
  fresh parsley
salt and pepper to taste

Optional:
few leaves fresh spinach,
  trimmed, washed, and
  chopped

1 Using a fine grater, grate the onion into a bowl.

2 Add the other ingredients and mix well.

3 Taste and correct the seasoning before refrigerating.

Makes about ½ cup

Horseradish and Mustard Sauce for Boiled Potatoes

This amount of sauce serves 6 to 10 people; the recipe can be halved to serve fewer people. It is especially good with corned beef and Galotsie Polonaise.

2 cups sour cream or yogurt
1–2 teaspoons horseradish
3 tablespoons finely chopped scallion

3 tablespoons Dijon mustard

1 Combine all the ingredients in a bowl.

2 Mix well.

3 Cover the bowl and refrigerate for 3 to 4 hours before serving.

Makes about 2¼ cups

White Sauce

Also called cream sauce or Béchamel sauce, this is a simple and basic sauce that lends itself to many variations. It is a standard way of refurbishing leftover chicken or vegetables. Substituting light or heavy cream for milk gives the sauce a richer flavor and texture; conversely, using skim milk or low-fat milk makes a serviceable sauce, and of course a healthier one. People on a low-cholesterol diet should substitute safflower or corn oil for the butter.

There are several schools of thought about cream sauce. Some cooks heat the milk before adding it to the flour and butter roux (the French term for the mixture of fat and flour). In that case, they add the heated milk all at once. Other cooks add cold milk gradually, stirring as they add. Still others use the top of a double boiler for the whole procedure. Aside from the question of method, proportions vary, using more or less of any of the three basic ingredients, depending on the thickness and richness desired.

With so much at stake, here are the ingredients.

2 tablespoons butter	*salt to taste*
2 tablespoons flour	
1 cup milk	**Optional:**
	pinch of nutmeg

1 Heat the milk but do not let it boil.

2 Meanwhile, melt the butter in a separate saucepan over low heat. Add the flour and stir for 1 minute with a wooden spoon or wire whisk. Keep the heat low so that the mixture does not burn.

3 Remove from heat, add the milk all at once, then return to the heat, stirring briskly. As the mixture comes to a boil, it will become thicker. Stir for a few minutes longer until it is smooth and moderately thick. Add the seasonings.

Variations: Add ⅓ cup grated Swiss or Cheddar cheese and you have cheese or Mornay sauce, which is good with broccoli, cauliflower, asparagus, hard-cooked eggs, ham, etc.

Substitute 1 cup of meat, chicken, or fish stock for the milk or cream and you have a Velouté, which is very useful as a base for soup.

Add an egg yolk to the white sauce and you have Sauce Allemande for eggs, chicken, or veal.

Note: If the sauce becomes lumpy, transfer it to the blender and blend for a second or two; then return it to the saucepan to heat gently for a few more minutes. If you have no blender, strain the sauce through a sieve and heat.

White Sauce for Pasta

This is the traditional Italian white sauce used for pasta. It is particularly good with green (or spinach) noodles or tortellini. This recipe is suitable for ½ pound of pasta.

½ stick butter
4 tablespoons grated
Parmesan cheese
4 tablespoons heavy
cream

salt and pepper to taste

1 Heat the butter in a saucepan over low heat.

2 Add the cheese and cream, stirring the mixture together until hot.

3 Season with salt and pepper before serving over well-drained cooked pasta.

Makes ¾ cup

Pesto alla Genovese

The Genoese invented pesto, a green sauce used with pasta or minestrone. Originally, the sauce was made with a mortar and pestle. In fact, pesto and pestle come from the same word, meaning to crush. The fresh basil leaves are crushed or pounded—these days in a blender or food processor, and perhaps the ease of making the sauce this way accounts for its popularity now. Pesto freezes well and can be stored in small containers if you wish to double or triple the recipe. If you have no fresh basil or fresh parsley, use a half-and-half combination of dried basil and dried parsley.

½ cup fresh basil leaves or 2 tablespoons dried basil and a good handful fresh parsley
¼ cup grated Parmesan or Romano cheese
1 cup olive oil

1 clove garlic, peeled
⅛ teaspoon salt
pepper to taste

Optional:
2 tablespoons pine nuts

1 Wash the basil or parsley. Place it with the cheese, nuts (if you like), garlic, salt and pepper in the blender or processor. Process at high speed (in the blender) until thoroughly blended.

2 Add the oil in a slow stream as you process, making sure that all the oil is incorporated and the mixture is homogenized.

3 Refrigerate or pour into small containers and freeze.

Makes about 1½ cups

Clam Sauce for Pasta

This sauce can be put together quickly while the pasta cooks. It makes enough for ¾ pound of pasta (2 to 3 servings) and is especially good with linguine.

6½-ounce can chopped clams
2 tablespoons olive oil
3 fresh tomatoes, blended, or peeled and chopped, or 14½-ounce can plum tomatoes, blended

2 cloves garlic, peeled and minced
⅛ teaspoon dried basil
salt and pepper to taste
2 tablespoons chopped fresh parsley

1 While the water for the pasta is boiling, drain the clams, emptying the juice into a stainless-steel or enameled saucepan. Add the olive oil, tomatoes, and seasonings (except for the parsley) to the clam juice and bring to a boil.

2 Simmer gently 15 to 20 minutes, uncovered.

3 Add the clams and parsley and simmer another 5 to 8 minutes.

Makes about 2 cups

Quick Tomato Sauce

This very pleasing quick sauce (adequate for ½ to ¾ pound of pasta—2 to 3 servings) can be made splendid by adding ⅓ cup light or heavy cream. It is good with shrimp and/or pasta.

1 small onion
3–4 fresh tomatoes* or a
    14½-ounce can plum
    tomatoes
2–3 tablespoons butter

½ teaspoon dried basil
salt to taste

Optional:
several capers

1 Chop the onion. In a stainless-steel or enameled saucepan, cook the onion, tomatoes, butter, and seasonings together over medium heat for 20 minutes.

2 In a blender or food processor, process the mixture until smooth.

3 Return to the saucepan and cook over medium heat, stirring, 5 to 10 minutes, until thick enough to coat the spoon. Add the capers if you wish.

Makes about 2 cups

  * See Introduction (page 15) for advice on tomatoes.

Spaghetti Sauce

This is enough sauce for ¾ pound of pasta—3 servings. It is best on spaghetti, vermicelli, and linguine and should be complemented by freshly grated Parmesan cheese.

2 tablespoons olive oil
½ pound ground beef
3 large fresh tomatoes or
   a 14½-ounce can plum
   tomatoes
   or preferably
Quick Tomato Sauce
   (page 184)

2 *cloves garlic, peeled*
   and minced
½ *teaspoon dried basil**
¼ *teaspoon dried oregano*
salt and pepper to taste
pinch of sugar

Optional:
   several Calamata olives,
     pitted and chopped

1 In a stainless-steel or enameled saucepan heat the olive oil; add the beef and garlic and sauté until well browned, about 5 minutes.

2 Blend the fresh or canned tomatoes, or add the Quick Tomato Sauce, and add to the sautéed ground beef. Add the seasonings and, if you wish, the chopped olives.

3 Bring to a boil, lower the heat, and simmer for 15 minutes. Season to taste.

Makes about 3 cups

* Omit if you use Quick Tomato Sauce.

Marinades for Shish Kebab

Here are five different marinades for Shish Kebab (see page 61). Each of them is distinctive, and each can be used as a basting sauce with roasted or broiled meats that are not skewered. Mix the ingredients of the marinade thoroughly. Pour over the meat to be marinated (in a nonmetallic bowl) and refrigerate overnight.

These are so simple to put up that they can be made freshly with very little trouble when you are ready to use any of them; there's no need to store them.

Greek

¼ cup olive oil
juice of 1 small lemon
¼ cup red wine

¼ teaspoon dried oregano
1 clove garlic, peeled and minced
salt and pepper to taste

Enough for ½ pound of meat

Russian

1 small onion, finely chopped
¼ cup red wine
¼ cup safflower or corn oil

1 clove garlic, peeled and minced
¼ teaspoon ground cinnamon
¼ teaspoon ground cloves
salt to taste
several crushed peppercorns

Optional:
2 tablespoons wine vinegar

Enough for ½ pound of meat

Armenian

half an 8-ounce can tomato
   sauce
¼ cup red wine
3 tablespoons olive oil

Enough for ½ pound of meat

¼ teaspoon mustard
   powder
¼ teaspoon Tabasco sauce
¼ teaspoon dried rosemary
salt and pepper to taste

Indian

½ cup yogurt
juice of 1 small lemon
2 tablespoons peanut, safflower, or corn oil
1 small onion, finely
   chopped

1 clove garlic, peeled
   and crushed
½ teaspoon dried mint
   leaves
¼ teaspoon freshly grated
   ginger
¼ teaspoon powdered
   cumin
¼ teaspoon ground
   cardamom
¼ teaspoon mace
¼ teaspoon turmeric
salt and pepper to taste

Enough for ½ pound of meat

Marinade for a Party

This is a splendid marinade, suitable for a whole leg of lamb that has been cubed for a party for 8 to 10 guests.

2 cups wine vinegar
¼ cup olive oil
4 large onions, chopped
4 cups Burgundy

1 *tablespoon salt*
1 *scant teaspoon sugar*
2 *dried bay leaves*
8 *whole cloves*
2 *pinches dried rosemary*
2 *pinches dried oregano*
2 *cloves garlic, peeled and minced*

1 In a nonaluminum saucepan gently heat the vinegar and spices. Do not boil. Remove from the heat and add the oil. Mix well.

2 In a large bowl, place part of the cubed lamb over a layer of chopped onions and garlic. Add another layer of chopped onions and garlic, another layer of lamb, and repeat the layering until all the meat is in place. Pour the marinade over the whole mound. Pour the wine over the contents of the bowl.

3 Place the bowl with the marinating lamb in the refrigerator, cover it tightly, and leave it for a week before broiling on skewers.

Makes 6¼ cups, enough for 1 leg of lamb

Sweet and Sour Barbecue Sauce

Use this as a marinade or a sauce for grilling. It is good on chicken, duck, shrimp, and pork—especially spare ribs, and is enough for 1 to 1½ pounds of meat.

½ lemon
¼ cup cider vinegar
½ cup honey

½ teaspoon freshly grated ginger
1 small clove garlic, peeled and minced
½ teaspoon mustard powder

Optional:
¼ cup canned crushed pineapple, drained, or canned apricots, peaches, or plums, pitted, drained and mashed with a fork

1 Squeeze the lemon.

2 Using a nonmetallic bowl, add the lemon juice, vinegar and seasonings to the honey. (Include the fruit if you like.)

3 Mix well.

Makes 1¼ to 1½ cups

Herb Butter

Excellent for small open sandwiches and crackers or with radishes; also as an accompaniment to steak, fish, or plain steamed vegetables. Have the butter at room temperature and use fresh herbs if you possibly can, being sure to wash out the sand and shake the herbs dry. If you use dried herbs, use ⅓ the amounts given below; but try at least to use fresh parsley.

1 stick butter
2 teaspoons lemon juice

1 small bunch watercress, chopped, or a combination of the following:
1 tablespoon chopped fresh parsley
1 tablespoon chopped fresh chives
2 teaspoons chopped fresh chervil or tarragon

1 Blend all the ingredients together in a food processor or with a fork, mashing and stirring.

2 Leave at room temperature 2 to 3 hours so that the flavors can blend.

3 Store in a covered jar in the refrigerator and use within a week.

Makes about ½ cup

Oriental Sauce for Stir-Frying

See the recipe for Chinese Stir-Fried Beef and Vegetables (page 62), which uses this sauce.

2 tablespoons tamari or soy sauce
1 tablespoon sweet or dry sherry
½ teaspoon honey or brown sugar
1 teaspoon cornstarch to thicken

1 clove garlic, peeled and minced
¼ teaspoon freshly grated ginger

1 Combine all the ingredients in a small bowl and mix thoroughly.

2 Add the sauce just at the end of the stir-frying procedure after the ingredients are cooked. Mix well.

3 Continue to stir for about 3 minutes and serve hot.

Note: If vegetables are added, allow this quantity of sauce (about 4 tablespoons of sauce) for every ½ pound of vegetables.

Makes enough for ½ pound of meat or vegetables

Fresh Cranberry Relish

This is an excellent accompaniment to pork and chicken as well as turkey; adding the optional bourbon will give it a longer shelf-life in the refrigerator. Use this recipe to prepare Sweet and Sour Pork Chops (page 57) and Cranberry-Raspberry Ice Cream (page 216).

2 cups fresh cranberries
1 orange
1 cup sugar

Optional:
½ jigger bourbon

1 Pick over the cranberries, discarding any that look questionable. Wash well. Cut the orange into quarters and remove the pits.

2 Place the cranberries in a blender or food processor, ½ cup at a time. Process and empty them into a bowl.

3 Blend the orange with the last ½ cup of cranberries and empty the mixture into the bowl. Pour the sugar (and bourbon) over the berries and mix well. Refrigerate.

Makes about 2½ cups

GRAINS

Kasha, or Buckwheat Groats

Kasha is prepared in much the same way as is the rice in the preceding recipe for pilaf: first it is roasted to separate the grains, then hot stock is added to swell the grains. But instead of being sautéed in oil, kasha is roasted with an egg.

2 cups beef or
  chicken stock
1 cup kasha
1 egg

salt to taste

1 Heat the stock.

2 Heat a heavy saucepan over medium heat for 2 minutes and add the kasha. Raise the heat to medium-high, and using a wooden spoon, stir the kasha for a minute or two so that it doesn't burn.

3 Add an unbeaten egg and stir it into the kasha. Keep stirring for 3 minutes, or until the grains look separate. Add the boiling stock, reduce the heat, and cover. Simmer for 15 minutes, or until all the liquid is absorbed. Check the liquid from time to time so that the kasha doesn't burn.

Variation: A medium-sized onion and/or a half dozen large mushrooms, chopped or sliced and sautéed in a separate pan, can be added at the end to make the kasha even better.

Serves 4

Rice Pilaf

The basic method for pilaf given here seems to produce fewer failures than does the conventional boiling of rice. Just be sure that the stock is boiling before you add it to the sautéed grains of rice. The sweet flavor of this dish (plus the addition of raisins during cooking if you wish) is a Middle Eastern variation that is especially good with chicken and lamb.

2 tablespoons butter or safflower or corn oil
1 cup long-grain rice
2 cups chicken stock or water

½ teaspoon ground cinnamon
¼ teaspoon dried oregano
¼ teaspoon ground coriander
½ teaspoon sugar
½ teaspoon salt

Optional:
¼ cup golden raisins
1 strip orange zest
pine nuts or almonds or sesame seeds for garnishing

1 In a skillet, heat the butter; add the raw rice and sauté for a few minutes over medium-high heat, stirring constantly with a wooden spoon.

2 Meanwhile, bring the stock or water to a boil. Pour the boiling stock over the rice and add the seasonings (and the raisins and/or orange zest if you wish).

3 Lower the heat. Cover the pot and simmer 12 to 15 minutes, or until the liquid has been absorbed. If desired, garnish with pine nuts, almonds, or sesame seeds.

Note: The method given here can be adapted to brown rice,

barley, and bulgur wheat. Just be sure to check the directions on the package for amounts of liquid and the cooking time. (See page 68 for information on cooking bulgur wheat.)

Serves 4

Respectably Refurbished Leftover Rice

This is a good recipe to know about when you're confronted with a dish of cold rice. It works just as well with barley, bulgur, or kasha.

2 cups cooked rice
2 ounces strong-tasting
   hard cheese (provolone,
   sharp Cheddar, or
   Swiss)
½ cup chicken or
   beef stock

½–1 teaspoon Tabasco
   or picante sauce
salt and pepper to taste

1 Stir the rice with a fork to break up any clumps. Place in a skillet or saucepan with a lid. Cut the cheese into small pieces.

2 Pour the stock over the rice, stir, and add the seasonings. Dot with the cheese.

3 Cover and cook on very low heat for about 15 minutes.

Serves 4

Egg Noodles

This recipe can be adapted to any pasta. Although it is not the Italian way of preparing it, it produces a rich, creamy taste without the use of cream—a boon to low-cholesterol dieters.

Just be sure to boil the noodles or pasta a shorter time than usual—even before the al dente point (see page 279) because the noodles will be boiled further in milk.

½ pound egg noodles
⅔ cup milk
½ cup small-curd cottage
    cheese

salt and pepper to taste

Optional:
½–1 teaspoon poppy seeds

1 Cook the noodles at least 2 minutes less than the directions on the package indicate. Drain well.

2 Return the noodles to the pot and add the remaining ingredients. Cook over medium heat, about 5 minutes, stirring constantly until the milk is almost absorbed and the cottage cheese is melted.

3 Season to taste, adding poppy seeds if desired, and serve.

Serves 4

Cornmeal Pudding, or Polenta

What follows is the Italian method of using cornmeal—in a pudding usually served with sausage or chicken livers or tomato sauce.

There is more than one way of cooking polenta. The fastest way (as in the following recipe) calls for beginning with a paste of cornmeal and cold water, then plunging it into boiling water. Some cooks use a double boiler; others use the oven. Most cooks simply pour the cornmeal slowly into boiling salted water, a method that requires longer cooking and stirring. No matter what the method, boiled polenta must be stirred with a wooden spoon as single-mindedly as possible in order to produce a perfectly smooth texture.

½ cup yellow cornmeal
⅓ cup cold water and 1½ cups boiling water
½ cup grated cheese (Parmesan or diced provolone)

⅓ *teaspoon salt*

Optional:
1 tablespoon butter to be added with the cheese

1 Mix the cornmeal, cold water, and salt.

2 Add to a large pot of boiling water and cook 10 minutes, stirring hard and steadily, until the mixture thickens.

3 Add the cheese and the butter, if you wish, and mix well. Serve at once: polenta should be eaten very hot.

Serves 2

Fried Bread

This is a standard accompaniment to bacon, eggs, and tomatoes for a full-fledged British breakfast. Fried bread cooked in olive oil rather than bacon fat is an excellent accompaniment to chicken, eggs, or soup and a useful substitute for grains, pasta, or potatoes.

2 slices good-quality white sandwich bread
2–3 tablespoons olive oil
1 tablespoon grated Parmesan cheese

1 Cut each slice of bread diagonally in half. Trim the crust if you wish.

2 Heat the oil in a skillet and fry the triangles on one side for a few minutes. Turn each triangle and sprinkle with Parmesan cheese.

3 Drain on paper towels laid out on a large plate. Serve at once or keep warm in the oven until serving time.

Serves 2

FOUR-INGREDIENT RECIPES

Low-Cholesterol Yorkshire Pudding

Yorkshire pudding is easily made, and its appearance—puffy and golden—is both impressive and comforting at the dinner table. In this recipe the polyunsaturated oil substitutes for beef drippings. You may find you like this version even better than the real thing.

2 eggs
1 cup milk
1 cup flour
¼ cup safflower or corn oil

½ teaspoon salt

Preheat the oven to 450°.

1 Grease a deep ovenproof dish, about 8 inches in diameter.

2 Pour the first three ingredients, in the order given, into the blender, and blend until well mixed.

3 Pour the oil into the baking dish and then pour in the batter. Bake 10 minutes, then reduce the heat to 350° and bake 15 to 20 minutes. The pudding should puff up and brown slightly. Serve immediately.

Serves 4

Scotch Scones

This recipe calls for a round shape called a bannock, though if you prefer, you may roll out the dough and cut it into squares or circles. Whatever shape you decide on, serve the finished scones with plenty of unsalted butter (dieters may prefer low-cholesterol margarine), honey, preserves (strawberry and peach are very good), or bitter orange marmalade. Excellent with tea.

1 cup self-rising flour
1 tablespoon sugar
½–⅔ cup buttermilk or light cream
⅛ cup dark or golden raisins or currants

Preheat the oven to 325°.

1 Sift the flour and sugar into a bowl, add the buttermilk or cream, and mix together to make a rather wet dough, adding a little more liquid if necessary.

2 Add the raisins or currants and mix again.

3 Place the dough on a lightly greased 9-inch pie plate. Spread the dough so that it fills the plate evenly and looks about ½ inch thick. With a floured table knife, cut it into 6 or 8 wedges, making sure not to cut all the way through. Bake 30 to 35 minutes. Remove from the oven and cut into wedges. Serve hot.

Serves 6 to 8

Appalachian Corn Bread

This recipe comes from eastern Kentucky but tastes a good deal like a splendid and chewy Mexican corn tortilla—it's so good you may want to double the recipe.

½ cup yellow cornmeal
½ cup flour
1½ teaspoons baking
  powder
1 cup water

½–¾ teaspoon salt

Preheat the oven to 400°. Preheat a well-oiled 10½-inch cast-iron skillet on a burner.

1 Mix all the ingredients together thoroughly and pour into the skillet.

2 Let cook on medium-high heat for 1 minute.

3 Place the skillet in the oven and bake 20 minutes. Remove and let cool slightly. Serve in wedges.

Serves 2 generously

Irish Soda Bread

You will know when this simple bread is done: it will sound hollow if you tap it with your knuckles. For a hard crust, stand the loaf on its side. For a soft crust, wrap it in a light towel to cool. In either case, cool it before cutting.

2 cups flour
2 teaspoons baking
  powder
¼ teaspoon baking soda
1 cup buttermilk

¾ *teaspoon salt*

Preheat the oven to 350°.

1 Mix the dry ingredients and add the buttermilk. The dough should be soft. Do not overmix.

2 Turn it out on a lightly floured board and knead for 1 minute. Shape the dough into a round loaf about 8 inches in diameter.

3 Place it in a greased round pan or on a greased cookie sheet. With a sharp knife, cut a cross on the top. Bake 40 to 50 minutes. Remove from the pan and let cool for about 15 minutes on a rack.

Makes 1 loaf

DESSERTS

Instant Fresh Applesauce

This method requires no cooking. The pulverized apple peel imparts a very fresh flavor to this unconventional applesauce.

2 medium-sized tart apples
⅓ cup water
2 teaspoons sugar

⅛ teaspoon ground
  cinnamon

1 Core and slice the apples. Do not peel.

2 Place the water in the blender jar and add half the apple slices and the sugar. Blend; then add the other half together with the cinnamon.

3 Keep blending until all the peel is processed and you have a smooth and perfectly homogenized applesauce.

Serves 2

Elevated Applesauce

The friend responsible for this wonderful improvement over applesauce has named it well. The blending of flavors produces a very fresh and delicate effect.

4 tablespoons orange juice
4 tablespoons buttermilk, yogurt, or sour cream
2 cups applesauce

¼ teaspoon almond extract
¼ teaspoon vanilla extract

1 Add the orange juice, buttermilk, and flavorings to the applesauce.

2 Stir well.

3 Chill at least 4 hours: the colder, the better. After refrigerating, you may place the applesauce in the freezer for 20 minutes before serving.

Serves 2 generously

Frozen Grapes and Yogurt

This recipe and the following one are basically combinations of fruit and yogurt. Both are far better than any commercial mixture, even the most natural. Each of these recipes is lovely and unusual and can be used for a company dinner.

½ pound green seedless grapes, washed and frozen
1 cup plain yogurt
2 teaspoons honey, or to taste

1 Put the grapes in the freezer for 3 hours until frozen.

2 Mix the yogurt and the honey.

3 Alternate layers of this mixture with frozen grapes in stemmed glasses or parfait glasses.

Serves 2

Glazed Bananas

This recipe can be made in the oven or in a frying pan on top of the stove. Either way, the bananas are wonderful with ice cream and chopped pecans.

2 firm but ripe bananas, peeled
2 tablespoons butter or margarine
2 tablespoons light brown sugar

Optional:
3 *tablespoons sweet sherry or rum*

OVEN METHOD

1 Heat the oven to 350°. Butter a baking dish or a cast-iron skillet.

2 Cut each banana lengthwise and dot each half with butter and brown sugar. Sprinkle with sherry if you wish.

3 Bake about 20 minutes, or until the bananas look nicely glazed.

SKILLET METHOD

1 Melt the butter over medium-high heat.

2 Cut each banana lengthwise and sprinkle with brown sugar and sherry, if you wish.

3 Sauté for 8 to 10 minutes, turning carefully with a spatula as soon as the sugar begins to caramelize (melt and turn into a light brown syrup). Remove from pan when both sides are light brown.

EASIEST METHOD OF ALL

2 firm but ripe bananas, unpeeled
1 tablespoon confectioners' sugar
½ lime

Preheat the oven to 350°.

1 Place the bananas in their peels in a pie pan.

2 Bake for 15 minutes. The skins will turn black.

3 Remove each banana to a plate. Peel away a strip of the skin the entire length of the banana, leaving it fastened at the bottom. Arrange attractively on a plate. Sprinkle the bananas with confectioners' sugar and garnish each with a wedge of lime.

Serves 2

Oranges in Wine

2 large navel oranges
¾ cup port wine or Dubonnet
2 teaspoons confectioners' sugar

1 Peel the oranges and slice them very thinly with a sharp (preferably serrated) knife.

2 Place the slices in a bowl and add the wine, making sure all the orange slices are submerged.

3 Sprinkle with the sugar, mix, and cover the bowl. Chill for several hours before serving.

Serves 4

Lychees and Yogurt

Lychees, a delicate and strange fruit, have become less exotic now that they are available in the Oriental section of many supermarkets. The following combination is particularly good.

2 cups plain yogurt
2 tablespoons light brown
   sugar
20-ounce can lychees, well
   chilled

1 *teaspoon vanilla extract*

Optional:
a sprinkling of chopped
   nuts

1 Mix the yogurt, brown sugar, and vanilla.

2 Drain the lychees and stir into the yogurt.

3 Chill and serve in stemmed glasses. Garnish with nuts, if you wish.

Serves 4 to 6

Preserved Kumquats

Kumquats appear around Christmastime in local supermarkets. If you buy several boxes and cook them, you can have not only an unusual dessert for yourself but a very welcome homemade gift for neighbors and friends.

1½ cups sugar
1½ cups water
1-quart box kumquats

Optional:
half-jigger rum, bourbon,
  or cognac

1 Boil the sugar and water 5 minutes in a saucepan. Let cool.

2 Meanwhile, wash the kumquats, removing all the leaves and discarding any green or shriveled fruit.

3 Place the kumquats in the cooled sugar-water syrup. Cover the pan, bring to a boil, and simmer about 1 hour. Remove the pot from the heat and do *not* remove the lid. Allow the contents of the pot to cool. Add the rum.

Note: For dessert, serve the kumquats in stemmed glasses with whipped cream (see page 273) or vanilla ice cream.

As a gift, place in small mason jars and refrigerate. Kumquats will last through the Christmas season in jars that have not been sterilized.

Serves 4 to 6

Glazed Pears

This recipe can be adapted to other fruit—pineapple slices, apple slices, peach halves, etc. It is good served with vanilla ice cream or whipped cream.

2 **Bartlett or Anjou pears**
2 **tablespoons butter**
2 **tablespoons light brown or granulated sugar**

Optional:
2 *tablespoons brandy (preferably apricot), kirsch, or sweet sherry*

1 Peel, cut in half, and core the pears.

2 Melt the butter in a skillet; add the pears and sauté until lightly browned.

3 Sprinkle with sugar, and after a few minutes, turn the pears gently to glaze well on both sides. If you wish, pour the brandy over the fruit and heat thoroughly, a minute or two.

Serves 2

Zabaglione

This fortified custard is a traditional Italian dessert, but there seem to be almost as many ways of preparing it as there are dialects in Italy. The following method produces a very good zabaglione.

2 egg yolks
2 teaspoons sugar
2 tablespoons Marsala or
   sweet sherry

Optional:
*bits of orange, lemon, or
   lime zest*

1 Place the egg yolks in the top of a double boiler and add the sugar. Beat steadily with a hand-held beater for a few minutes.

2 Add the Marsala (and citrus zest, if you wish) and beat again.

3 Now pour about 2 inches of boiling water in the lower part of the double boiler, placing it over medium heat. Put the top in position and, beating constantly, cook the egg mixture until it thickens. Do not allow to boil. Serve warm or at room temperature in stemmed glasses.

Variation: Place chilled fruit at the bottom of a stemmed glass, pour zabaglione over it, and garnish with a little more fruit.

Serves 2

Creamy Rice Pudding

Middle Eastern cooks have traditionally pounded the grains of raw rice with a mortar and pestle to produce a smooth and creamy texture. Pulverizing the rice in a blender does the same thing, and either method considerably shortens the cooking time. Rosewater, a wonderful alternate flavoring to vanilla and orange peel, can usually be obtained at a pharmacy.

1½ cups milk
¼ cup rice
⅛–¼ cup sugar (depending on taste)

1 teaspoon rosewater
   or
½ teaspoon vanilla extract and ½ teaspoon grated orange peel
pinch of salt

1 Place the milk, rice, and sugar in a blender and process until the rice is pulverized.

2 Place the mixture in the top of a double boiler and heat, uncovered, over simmering water for 1½ hours or until all the liquid has been absorbed.

3 Add the flavorings and cook a little longer.

Note: Check from time to time to make sure the bottom of the double boiler contains enough water.

Serves 3

Graham Cracker Crust

These 3 ingredients are all you need for your own pie crust—and it will be far superior in flavor to the commercial variety and will contain fewer additives. You can vary the recipe by using crumbs made in the blender or food processor from vanilla wafers, chocolate wafers, or gingersnaps.

5 tablespoons butter
1¼ cups graham cracker crumbs (9 whole crackers or 18 squares)
¼ cup brown sugar

1 Melt the butter over low heat.

2 Mix the graham cracker crumbs with the brown sugar. Add the melted butter and mix well.

3 Press the mixture onto the bottom and sides of a 9-inch pie plate. Either chill the crust well or bake at 350° for 10 minutes.

Makes a 9-inch pie crust

Nut Crust

Another alternative to pastry crust, this is very good for pies with frozen fillings (like ice cream, frozen Quick Mocha Mousse, or Chocolate Ricotta Frozen Dessert).

1 egg white
2 cups ground nuts (pecans, walnuts, almonds, or hazelnuts)
2 tablespoons dark brown sugar

1 teaspoon freshly grated nutmeg
1 teaspoon grated orange or lemon zest

Preheat the oven to 300°.

1 Beat the egg white until frothy.

2 Combine all the ingredients and mix until they adhere, but avoid overmixing.

3 Press into a greased pie plate. Bake 10 to 15 minutes. Remove from the oven, and when cool, fill with filling and freeze.

Makes an 8- or 9-inch pie crust

Crumb Topping or Streusel

A useful thing to know about if you are baking a pie with only a bottom crust and you want something more on top. It is an excellent topping for baked fruit, especially apples.

6 tablespoons flour
½ cup light brown sugar
4 tablespoons butter

½ teaspoon ground
  cinnamon

Optional:
⅓ cup chopped almonds,
  pecans, walnuts or
  hazelnuts

1 Mix all the ingredients with your hands, but do not over-work: the mixture should be crumblike.

2 Spread over sliced fruit or the pie filling.

3 Bake at 375° as a topping for fruit, or use the temperature setting directed for the pie, for about 30 minutes or until the fruit is tender.

Makes enough for an 8- or 9-inch pie or oven dish filled with fruit

Cranberry-Raspberry Ice Cream

This is an unexpected and very refreshing combination, particularly after a hearty meal like Corned Beef and Cabbage or Galotsie Polonaise.

1 cup Cranberry Relish (page 192)
1 cup frozen raspberries, thawed
2 scoops vanilla ice cream

1 Place all the ingredients in the blender.

2 Blend briefly until they are thoroughly incorporated.

3 Transfer to a freezer dish for an hour or so, until the ice cream reaches a firm but malleable state. Serve in stemmed glasses.

Serves 2 generously

Frozen Berry Cream

This simple and delicious dessert should be served chillingly cold but not solidly frozen: if you remove it from the freezer at the beginning of the meal, it ought to be just the right temperature and consistency.

8-ounce container whipping cream
10-ounce box frozen strawberries (in syrup), defrosted
10-ounce box frozen raspberries (in syrup), defrosted

1 Pour the cream into the blender and blend for a few seconds or until the cream begins to thicken. Add the berries. Blend about 1 minute, or until thoroughly mixed and thickened, but do not overblend.

2 Pour into a plastic dish and put in the freezer.

3 Remove after 2 hours and stir well to break up the ice crystals forming. Refreeze for 2 more hours.

Variation: For raspberry lovers, follow the recipe above, substituting a second box of frozen raspberries for the strawberries. This dessert can also be made using frozen blueberries or blackberries; but because these berries are marketed without added sugar, you will have to add confectioners' sugar, according to taste, to sweeten them.

Serves 6 to 8

Quick Mocha Mousse

It would be more accurate to call this dish a fool rather than a mousse since it dispenses with the raw eggs called for in the traditional mousse. This dessert, so simple and satisfying to lovers of chocolate and whipped cream, should be made with real chocolate morsels, not the chocolate-flavored kind.

3 ounces semisweet choc-
    olate bits (½ of a 6-
    ounce package)
1 teaspoon instant coffee,
    preferably espresso
½ cup heavy cream

½ teaspoon ground
    cinnamon

1 Melt the chocolate in the top of a double boiler over simmering water. When the chocolate melts, add the coffee, cinnamon, and 1 teaspoon of water. Stir well. Remove the mixture from the heat and allow it to cool.

2 Whip the cream (see page 273).

3 Fold the cream into the chocolate mixture. Divide the mousse between 2 stemmed glasses and chill for several hours.

Serves 2

Chocolate Ricotta Frozen Dessert

This is a good recipe for people who cannot or should not have cream or eggs in their diet. It can be served as a frozen dessert, slightly softened.

4 ounces semisweet chocolate
1 pound ricotta cheese*
¼–½ cup light brown sugar, depending on taste

1 teaspoon vanilla extract
slivers of orange and lemon zest

Optional:
½ teaspoon almond extract

1 Melt the chocolate in the top of a double boiler over simmering water. Allow the chocolate to cool.

2 Combine the ricotta cheese, brown sugar, and vanilla (and the almond extract, if you wish) in the blender and blend until the mixture is perfectly smooth.

3 Add the chocolate and the peel to the blender and blend again. Pour the mixture into a freezer container and chill in the refrigerator for 2 hours. Stir and refreeze for 1 or 2 more hours.

Variation: To make a Chocolate Ricotta Pie, pour the mixture in Step 3 into a Graham Cracker Crust (see page 213) or a Nut Crust (see page 214) and chill 3 to 4 hours.

Serves 6

* You may substitute creamed cottage cheese, but it won't be quite as good.

Iced Coffee with Ice Cream

This mocha concoction is rich enough—and good enough—to substitute for dessert-and-coffee. For best results, brew fresh strong coffee in your coffeemaker and let it cool. You can use instant coffee if necessary.

2 cups freshly brewed coffee
2 scoops chocolate ice cream
¼ cup milk or light cream

Optional:
4 ice cubes

1 Pour the coffee into the blender jar.

2 Add the ice cream and milk (and the ice cubes, if you wish). Blend well.

3 Pour into large glasses and serve.

Serves 2

Hot Brandied Apricot Sauce

This can be poured over crêpes, pancakes, ice cream, or pound cake.

½ cup apricot preserves
⅓ cup apricot juice
2–3 tablespoons good brandy or Grand Marnier

1 Heat the preserves until they reach the boiling point.

2 Add the apricot juice and mix well.

3 Add the brandy and mix. Pour into a small pitcher and serve.

Makes about 1 cup

Bitter Chocolate Sauce

This sauce can be used hot or cold over ice cream, crêpes, pancakes, or plain cake.

4 ounces unsweetened chocolate
½ cup pure maple syrup
½ cup light cream

1 Place the ingredients in the top of a double boiler.

2 Cook slowly, stirring from time to time.

3 When the chocolate is melted and the sauce seems smooth, it is ready to be served.

Makes 1½ cups

Cream Cheese Icing

A quick, attractive, and not too sugary frosting that is very suitable for cupcakes or a cake for a child's party.

8-ounce package Philadelphia cream cheese
½ large juice orange
2–3 tablespoons confectioners' sugar

1 Squeeze 2 tablespoons orange juice and grate enough orange rind, using the fine side of the grater, to fill 2 teaspoons.

2 With an electric beater or in a food processor, beat the cream cheese until fluffy.

3 Add the sugar and mix well.

Makes enough for 1-layer 8-inch round cake or 12 cupcakes

Chocolate Cups for Ice Cream

This striking dessert is easily made using cupcake papers and the chocolate cups are then filled with ice cream.

9 ounces semisweet chocolate bits (1½ 6-ounce packages or 1½ cups)
3 tablespoons butter
6 cupcake papers

Optional:
chopped almonds, pecans, walnuts, hazelnuts

1 Melt the chocolate and butter in the top of a double boiler over boiling water. Mix well and, if you wish, add nuts.

2 Arrange the cupcake papers in a muffin tin. Coat the inside of each paper with about a tablespoon of the chocolate, using the back of a spoon to spread the chocolate. Refrigerate.

3 When well chilled, peel the paper away from the chocolate. Fill the chocolate cups with ice cream and garnish with chopped nuts if you like.

Note: If you wish to use contrasting flavors of ice cream, follow the same method but use paper nutmeat cups or petit four cases to make tiny chocolate cups. Fill each with a different flavor of ice cream and place three on a plate.

Makes 6

Forgotten Torte

This is a recipe that friends love to give one another: anything that can cook while we sleep is particularly appealing. This soft meringue bakes overnight in a gradually cooling oven. It can be served with sugared fruit (raspberries, strawberries, peaches) spooned over it, topped by a layer of whipped cream, or it can be filled with ice cream and chocolate sauce or Quick Mocha Mousse (triple the recipe on page 218).

6 egg whites at room
   temperature
½ teaspoon cream of
   tartar

1½ cups sugar
¼ teaspoon salt
1 teaspoon vanilla extract

Preheat the oven to 450° for 45 minutes.

1 While the oven is heating, beat the egg whites together with the cream of tartar and salt until stiff peaks form. (See page 274 for information on beating egg whites.)

2 Add the sugar and vanilla very slowly and beat until stiff and glossy.

3 Pour the mixture into a well-greased 10-inch quiche pan. Turn the oven off and immediately place the pan inside. (Be sure not to place the meringue in the oven until it is turned off.) Allow *no one* to open the oven door. Remove the meringue from the oven the next morning.

Serves 6

Bløtkake

This seemingly ominous word translates into whipped cream cake. This is a classic Norwegian dessert—universally loved. It would be hard to find a restaurant in Norway that did not include it on the menu.

One of the virtues of this recipe is that an inexperienced baker—or nonbaker—who follows it can produce an absolutely professional-looking cake. Another is that it requires no baking—no hot ovens in the summer. The recipe can, of course, be adapted to any plain homemade cake that would normally be frosted and that is compatible with the fruit you choose. Yellow cake or angel food cake would work well. If you do bake your own, you'll need two layers.

8-ounce container whipping cream
1 Sara Lee frozen pound cake
20-ounce can sliced pineapple*

Optional:
3–4 tablespoons sweet sherry or rum

1 Whip the cream. (See page 273 for the rule.)

2 Cut the cake in half horizontally (see page 268 for instructions). Pour ¼ cup of the liquid from the can over one layer and allow it to soak in. (You may want to use a few tablespoons of sherry or rum, in which case use less of the liquid.) Cover the layer with whipped cream. Then place as many slices of fruit as you can fit on the surface, overlapping if you need to.

3 Place the second layer over the first and repeat the process: juice, then whipped cream, then fruit. Be sure to arrange the fruit as artfully as you can.
Serves 8 to 10

* Other canned fruit can be substituted. Apricots, plums, and pears are probably the best to use.

Pecans Berkeley

Since these cookies contain no butter or margarine, by the wonderful logic of cookie-lovers one can eat them in unlimited quantity with a good conscience.

1 cup light brown sugar
1 egg white, beaten until stiff
2 cups pecans

1 teaspoon vanilla extract
pinch of salt

Preheat the oven to 325°.

1 Gradually add the brown sugar, then the vanilla and salt to the beaten egg white.

2 Stir in the pecans slowly so that all of them are coated with the egg white and sugar mixture.

3 Using 2 teaspoons (one to scoop up the batter, the other to scrape it off), drop the batter onto a well-oiled baking sheet (or one sprayed with Pam®). (Make sure the cookies do not overlap, since they spread in the course of baking.) Bake 15 minutes. Allow the cookies to cool for a few minutes before removing from the baking sheet or they may stick to the spatula.

Makes about 2 dozen cookies

FOUR-INGREDIENT RECIPES

Cherries Jubilee

This is a showy dessert. It is at its best prepared at the table in a chafing dish, but it can also be prepared in the kitchen in a saucepan.

16-ounce can pitted dark sweet cherries
1 tablespoon cornstarch
¼ cup + 2 tablespoons cognac, divided
6 servings vanilla ice cream

1 Drain the cherries and place them in a bowl, reserving the juice. Cover the cherries with ¼ cup cognac and stir.

2 Mix the cornstarch with ½ cup of the cherry juice. Pour it into a chafing dish or saucepan and heat, stirring until thick.

3 Add the cherries and cognac, stir, and heat through. Add 2 more tablespoons of cognac and light the sauce with a match, averting your face. Serve the sauce over vanilla ice cream.

Serves 6

Pears with Cointreau

A delicate dessert, perfect after a rich meal. If you want a richer dessert, simply pass whipped cream and a dish of whole toasted almonds.

¼ cup sugar
2 pears
juice of ½ lemon
1 jigger Cointreau

1 Add the sugar to 2 cups of water and bring to a boil. Boil for 5 minutes. Meanwhile, peel and core the pears and cut them into wedges. Sprinkle with lemon juice.

2 Add the pears to the syrup, lower the heat, and cook gently 5 minutes or longer, until the fruit is tender (easily pierced with a fork).

3 Pour the fruit and the syrup into a serving bowl and let cool. Add the Cointreau, cover, and refrigerate for several hours.

Serves 2

Pineapple Sherbet

Very refreshing, no trouble at all, and very good for you—high in calcium, low in fat.

20-ounce can crushed pineapple
2 lemons
1 quart buttermilk
¾ cup honey

1 Drain the pineapple.

2 Grate the rind of 1 lemon. Squeeze the juice as well as the juice of the remaining lemon.

3 Mix all the ingredients together. Place in a freezer container and freeze. Remove from the freezer after 2 hours and stir to break up the ice crystals. Refreeze and repeat after 2 more hours.

Serves 12

Sweet Lemon Omelet

If you try this lovely dessert omelet—and you certainly should—it's a good idea to complete Step 1 before the meal begins, just to speed things up between courses.

4 eggs
3 teaspoons confectioners'
  sugar, divided
grated peel of 1 small
  lemon
2 tablespoons butter

1 teaspoon vanilla extract

1 Separate the egg yolks from the whites. Grate the lemon.

2 Using a hand-held electric beater, beat the egg whites to the soft-peak stage. Then beat the yolks until they thicken. Add the lemon peel, 2 teaspoons confectioners' sugar, and vanilla to the yolks, mixing well. Fold the whites into the yolks.

3 Heat the broiler. Heat a skillet over medium-high heat and melt the butter. Pour the egg mixture carefully into the hot butter and let it cook for a few minutes without stirring. Sprinkle with the remaining confectioners' sugar and finish under the broiler for a few minutes to cook the surface. Remove when the omelet is browned and puffy.

Serves 2

Tipsy Pudding

The more rum you pour over this other cake-like old English pudding, the tipsier it—or whoever eats it—will presumably be.

2 eggs
⅓–½ cup sugar
½ cup flour
½ cup or more light rum

Preheat the oven to 350°.

1 Beat the eggs in a bowl, gradually adding the sugar and beating until the mixture is lemon-colored and thick.

2 Sift the flour and add it to the eggs and sugar. Mix but do not beat.

3 Pour the mixture into an oiled 7- or 8-inch baking dish and bake 20 minutes, or until browned. Spoon the rum over the surface when the pudding has cooled.

Serves 2 generously

Sour Apple Pie, or Schnitz Pie

An Amish recipe using dried apples or *schnitz*, this is even simpler than apple pie, since the apples need no coring, peeling, or slicing.

2 unbaked 9-inch pie crusts, commercial or homemade
½ pound dried sour apples*
½ orange
1 cup sugar

1 tablespoon ground cinnamon
¼ teaspoon salt

Preheat the oven to 450°.

1 Cook the apples in 2 cups of water until you have a soft pulp. Drain the apples if necessary.

2 While they are cooking, grate the orange rind, using only the zest or orange part. Juice the orange.

3 Mix the apples with the orange juice, rind, sugar, and seasonings. Pour the mixture into one pie crust and cover the top with the second. Cut several slits in the top pastry to let the steam escape. Bake at 450° for 10 minutes, then lower the heat to 350° and cook 30 minutes longer.

Serves 6

* Obtainable in many health food stores.

Coconut Pie Filling

Surprisingly easy and delicious, this filling makes a perfect pie for non-pie-makers.

1 stick butter or
 margarine
3 eggs
¾ cup sugar
1 cup sweetened shredded
 coconut

1 teaspoon vanilla extract

Preheat the oven to 325°.

1 Melt the butter over low heat. Allow to cool. Meanwhile, beat the eggs.

2 Add the sugar and coconut to the melted butter and mix well. Add the beaten eggs and vanilla to the mixture and mix well again.

3 Pour the mixture into a Graham Cracker Crust (page 213) and bake for 45 minutes, or until a knife inserted comes out clean. If the top seems to be browning too quickly, cover it with foil. Allow to cool before serving.

Serves 6

Strawberry Pie Filling

This filling requires no baking. Just be sure you pour it into a pie crust that has already been baked or into one that requires no further baking (like a Graham Cracker Crust, page 213). You may of course substitute other kinds of berries or sliced peaches, or if you can find them, really ripe apricots.

8-ounce package cream cheese, at room temperature
⅓ cup sour cream
¼ cup sugar
1 quart fresh strawberries

confectioners' sugar to taste

1 Cream the cream cheese, sour cream, and granulated sugar.

2 Spread the mixture over the pie crust.

3 Wash and hull the strawberries. Slice them and sugar them with confectioners' sugar, mixing lightly. Distribute the berries over the cream cheese mixture and refrigerate.

Serves 6

Homemade Granola Fruit Bars

These need no baking and are best made with raspberry or apricot preserves although pineapple, strawberry, peach, or blueberry preserves are perfectly good substitutes.

2 tablespoons butter
18-ounce jar preserves
3 cups granola
3–4 tablespoons confectioners' sugar

1 Melt the butter in a saucepan and add the contents of the jar. Mix and cook over low heat. Using a candy thermometer, let the mixture cook until it reaches the softball stage (234° to 238°). If you have no thermometer, watch for the softball stage—after about 15 minutes—when the mixture is bubbling hard, and the whole surface is covered with bubbles.

2 Remove from the heat and let cool, about 10 minutes. Add the granola, mixing well.

3 Grease an 8-inch baking pan and dust it with half the confectioners' sugar, pressing the sugar through a tea strainer. Pour in the mixture. Dust with the rest of the strained sugar and cut into squares.

Makes 16 squares

Greek Shortbread, or Kourabiedes

These cookies are traditionally made for Christmas. This particular version calls for clarifying* the butter (so that the cookies literally melt in your mouth) and toasting the almonds to bring out their full flavor. The results are superb. What follows includes alternatives for readers who do not wish to take the time to clarify the butter or who must substitute a low-cholesterol margarine.

2½   sticks butter if butter is to be clarified or 2 sticks butter or margarine
¼   cup sugar
3   cups plus 3 tablespoons flour
2   ounces almonds, toasted† and coarsely chopped

Optional:
confectioners' sugar for dusting

Preheat oven to 325°.

1   Using an electric or manual beater, cream the butter and sugar until whitish and fluffy.

2   Add the flour and nuts to the creamed butter and sugar, working the mixture with your hands. Mix well.

3   Take a small handful of dough and knead it well, finally shaping it into rounds or ovals ½ inch thick. Place on an un-

---

* To clarify butter, melt it slowly, then, using a tablespoon, carefully skim off the white foam at the top. Pour the yellow portion through a small strainer, and you have clear, or clarified, butter. Before using it for this recipe, refrigerate, then use at room temperature.

† See page 276 for toasting nuts.

greased cookie sheet and bake 14 to 20 minutes. Remove when they begin to turn light brown: they should be more white than light brown. Transfer to a rack, cool, and dust with confectioners' sugar if you wish.

Makes about 3 dozen 1-inch round cookies

. . . And in case you're feeling adventurous, here's a recipe with a fifth ingredient:

Berliner Brot

More like cake, this "bread" refuses to be sweet in spite of the pound of brown sugar. Don't be alarmed at the stiffness of the dough. If you wish to add the almonds, punch them into the dough with your fingers. Berliner Brot is wonderful with coffee.

½ pound bitter chocolate
5 eggs
¼ teaspoon hartshorn*
4 scant cups flour
2½ cups firmly packed
  dark brown sugar

¼ *teaspoon ground cloves*
1 *teaspoon ground*
  cinnamon

Optional:
⅔ *cup shelled almonds*

Preheat the oven to 325°.

1 Grate the chocolate. Beat the eggs. Mix the chocolate and eggs.

2 Mix the hartshorn with the unsifted flour and add the sugar, cloves, and cinnamon. Add the dry ingredients to the chocolate and eggs. Mix well.

3 Coax—or push—the dough into an 8 by 12 inch oiled pan. Bake 35 to 40 minutes. Remove from oven and let cool 5 minutes. Turn out on rack to cool further. Slice when cool into strips 2 inches long and ¾ inch wide.

Makes about 5 dozen small slices

* This unexpected ingredient, also known as ammonium carbonate, can be obtained at a pharmacy.

DISHES FOR SPECIAL OCCASIONS

Cheese Straws for a Large Party

There is no version I know of that is better than this one. Unlike many other recipes for cheese straws, this one advises against grating the cheese. Instead, use a food processor or a meat grinder.

1 **pound good sharp Cheddar cheese**
3 **sticks margarine**
4 **cups flour**

3–4 drops Tabasco sauce

Preheat the oven to 325°.

1 Process or grind the cheese. Add the margarine and flour to the processor, or place the ingredients in a bowl and mix together with your hands. Do not use a mixer: it will make the mixture too fluffy. Mix until the dough acquires the texture of modeling clay—i.e., it holds the impression of your fingers but does not stick to them.

2 Pat out the dough into rectangles about 4 by 6 inches and ⅛ inch thick. Cut the rectangles with a dull knife into strips about as wide as the dough is thick.

3 Place on a baking sheet and bake about 10 to 12 minutes, until the cheese straws are golden and firm, but not hard. Watch that they do not burn, especially on the bottom. Remove from the heat and place crosswise on a rack to cool. Store in an airtight tin.
Makes enough for 20-30 people

Eggs Kiev

These are for a very special occasion and should be presented as attractively as possible on a leaf of Boston lettuce or a bed of shredded romaine, garnished with parsley and accompanied by melba toast.

6 eggs
⅓ cup sour cream
2-ounce jar lumpfish caviar

Optional:
finely minced onion or
scallion

1 Hard-cook the eggs (see page 276). Plunge them into a bowl of cold water and peel.

2 Carefully cut each egg in half vertically. Place a dollop of sour cream on each half.

3 Add a little mound of caviar. Sprinkle with onion or scallion if desired, and serve, allowing two halves per person.

Serves 6

Marinade for a Party—see recipe page 188.

Baked Beans for Twenty People

For this recipe you will need a bean pot and an alarm clock. If you set it for 6 A.M. on the morning of your party and put up the beans as soon as you can, they will be ready at about 8 P.M.,* and your house will be filled with the aroma of beans cooking in molasses and garlic. You can't know how good baked beans are until you taste these.

2 pounds navy beans
¾ cup molasses
½ pound dark brown sugar
¼ pound salt pork

2 large cloves garlic, peeled

1 Soak the beans overnight in a large pot of water to cover. In the morning, bring them to a boil and simmer for 1 hour. Drain well.

2 In a bean pot, place a 2-inch layer of beans, then pour about ¼ cup of molasses over them, and add 3 heaping tablespoons of brown sugar and the garlic.

3 Cut the salt pork into 1-inch cubes and divide into 3 portions. Add the first portion to the first layer of beans, and repeat the whole layering process twice—first the beans, then the molasses, sugar, and salt pork. Cover the bean pot and bake in a 250° oven for about 14 hours.

Serves 20

 * Another method—for late-risers—is simply to put up the beans the night before and let them bake until morning for a total of thirteen hours. In that case, before serving, add ½ cup of water to the beans without disturbing the layering and bake at 350° for 30 minutes.

Wedding "Pie"

A composite of three 3-ingredient recipes in three layers. You will need to calculate the amounts needed and do some multiplying or dividing. For example, to feed 20 guests, multiply the potato salad and the egg salad recipes by 10 and triple the caviar recipe. To serve 20, you will probably need more than one large dish.

Roman Potato Salad
  recipe (page 164)
Egg Salad recipe (page
  160)
Caviar Spread recipe (page
  26)

Optional:
minced scallions

1 Place a layer of potato salad in an attractive large deep dish (glass, if possible, so that you can see the layers).

2 Place a layer of egg salad over the potato salad. Sprinkle with minced scallions, if you wish.

3 Spread the cream cheese and sour cream mixture over the egg salad. Just before bringing the dish to the table, spread over the entire surface the contents of as many 2-ounce jars of black or red caviar as you need.

A Feast from the Oven

This idea originated when I found myself in a tiny kitchen in England, with only one baking pan (for the Sunday roast) and many guests. Whenever you have a chicken or a roast cooking in a 325° to 350° oven, you can make any or all of the following, as you wish (allow 1 per serving):

whole medium potatoes or
   yams, unpeeled but
   scrubbed
whole tomatoes, washed
whole apples, washed
whole medium onions,
   unpeeled

salt and pepper to taste

1 Place potatoes or yams, tomatoes, apples, and onions on pieces of aluminum foil and put them wherever they will fit in the oven. Use the timetable in Step 2.

2 Bake the potatoes or yams and onions for 1½ hours, the apples for 1 hour, and the tomatoes for the last 20 minutes.

3 When the onions are baked, slice off the root ends, squeeze the onions out of their skins, and serve with butter, salt, and freshly ground pepper. Arrange all the vegetables on a large platter around the roasted meat or poultry.

Galotsie Polonaise, a Polish Stew

(13 ingredients in one pot)

Here, finally, is a dish for those who feel deprived of ingredients. It can be made with very little trouble. Just keep adding the ingredients to one large ovenproof container, slicing whenever indicated.

1 pound boneless fresh pork, cut in slices
½ pound ham, cut in slices
1 pound bacon,* cut in pieces
½–¾ pound Polish sausage coarsely sliced
1 pound mushrooms, sliced
8-ounce bottle stuffed green olives
2 tablespoons butter
1 pound tomatoes, sliced, or a 16-ounce can tomatoes
16-ounce can sauerkraut, washed and drained
2 large apples, peeled, cored, and sliced
2 cups tomato juice
4 medium-sized onions, peeled and sliced
1 small green cabbage, sliced

4 bay leaves
salt and pepper to taste
1 teaspoon sugar

Preheat the oven to 375°.

$\mathbb{1}$ Combine all the ingredients in a large casserole and cook for 2 hours in the oven (or simmer in a large pot on top of the stove for 2 hours).

$\mathbb{2}$ Serve in the casserole directly from the oven (or transfer from the pot to a large platter). Spoon some sauce over each serving.

$\mathbb{3}$ Serve with small boiled potatoes accompanied by Horseradish and Mustard Sauce (page 179).

Serves 8 to 10

 * To reduce the amount of fat, boil the bacon in water, discard the water, and proceed.

LIST OF HERBS AND SPICES

allspice

A clovelike, peppery flavor; used in pickling vegetables and meats, with cooked fruit, in vegetable soups and sauces.

anise seed

A licorice-flavored spice; used in cookies and bread, in cooked fruit (apples, pears, peaches, pineapple), steamed fish, and mixed raw vegetable salads.

basil

A strong-flavored, strong-smelling herb with an anise-like and lemony flavor; used fresh or dried with fresh tomatoes and in tomato sauces, in soups and salad, with vegetables and chicken, and as the primary ingredient of Pesto (page 182); very compatible with garlic in soups and sauces.

bay leaf

One of the three main ingredients, along with parsley and thyme, of the *bouquet garni*; used in sauces, stock, stews, and soups, particularly in bean, lentil, or chick-pea soups; also in grilled meats on skewers.

caraway seed

A crunchy seed with a sharp and distinctive flavor; used with raw or cooked cabbage (very good in coleslaw) and potatoes (notably potato salad), in salad dressings, bread (particularly rye bread), cakes and cookies; the chief flavoring agent of kümmel, the German liqueur.

cardamom	Used in Indian cooking, particularly in curries and sweets, in apple pie, and in Scandinavian baked goods. The seeds are sometimes used whole but are more often pounded to a powder.
cayenne pepper	A hot and pungent powder made from the seeds of several hot peppers; to be used judiciously in fish chowder and seafood bisques, in sauces, dressings (particularly mayonnaise), and in egg dishes.
celery seed	A small seed used to lend celery flavor to soups, salad dressings, stews, and cooked vegetables (tomatoes, cabbage, peppers, and eggplant).
chervil	A parsley-like plant with a mild flavor that slightly recalls tarragon; one of the standard ingredients in *fines herbes*, along with parsley, chives, and tarragon; used in fish, egg, chicken, and veal dishes, in soups (particularly cream soups), in Béarnaise sauce, white sauce, and salad dressings.
chili peppers	These are hot. Obtainable dried (crushed or powdered) or fresh, they should be used with caution: if you're not fond of hot food, avoid them. (Dried chili peppers should be soaked in water and simmered for 20 minutes; the seeds and membranes should be discarded, as should the seeds and membranes of fresh chili peppers.)
chili powder	A powdered mixture of peppers with garlic, cumin, and oregano; used in chutneys, sharp tomato sauces, marinades, and, of course, in chili con carne.
chives	Slender green shoots with an oniony flavor; used in place of scallions or mild

onions in omelets and egg salads, in cottage cheese and cream cheese, in soups, sauces, stews, and in vegetable, meat, and seafood salads, or as a garnish.

cinnamon   Available in stick or powdered form; used in chocolate or honey sauces, with cooked fruit (apples, peaches, pears, bananas), in pickling solutions, with meat and chicken dishes in Middle Eastern and Indian cooking, with rice, in yeast cakes and cookies, and with coffee.

cloves   Available whole or ground; used with ham and chicken, fresh and cooked fruit, custards, cakes, cookies, in pickling solutions and marinades. (Whole cloves must be removed from the dish before serving.) An onion pierced with 4 to 6 cloves is commonly used in French cooking to flavor soups and stews.

coriander   A large-leafed parsley-like herb now widely available fresh under the name Chinese parsley, or the Spanish cilantro; the dried seeds of the plant are used to season pork and chicken dishes, particularly in Southeast Asian and Indian cooking; also used in cooked fruit and marinades.

cumin   Often used in powdered form with spinach, cucumbers, eggplant, rice, chicken and lamb dishes, and in soups, also in many North African, Indian, and Mexican dishes.

curry powder   A blend of many related spices, among them: allspice, cardamom, cayenne, chili, cinnamon, cloves, coriander, cumin, ginger, mace, mustard, nutmeg, black pepper, and turmeric. There is no one definitive blend, and the prepared powder can vary greatly, depending on which spices predominate. Used in soups, with vegetables, eggs, chicken, meat, fish, and shellfish. (Best in cooked rather than uncooked dishes.)

dillseed	The seed of the dill plant; used in pickling, fish sauces, vegetable soups, vegetable purees, meat stews, and salads.
dillweed	The chopped leaves of the dill plant; used with beets and cucumbers, in potato and egg salads, in dips, cold soups, and fish dishes. Fresh dill, preferable to the dried, is often available during the summer.
fennel	The seeds of the finocchio plant give a distinctive flavor to steamed fish, steamed or sautéed vegetables, beans, bean soups, salads, and rice.
ginger	Available fresh as ginger root or in powdered form; much used in stir-frying, also with poultry, cooked fruit, particularly pumpkin, and, of course, in gingerbread. Store fresh ginger in the freezer.
mace	Mace and nutmeg come from the same plant and are similar in flavor. Ground for seasoning, mace is a standard ingredient in curry powders; its fragrance makes it particularly good in cooked desserts.
marjoram	A fragrant and spicy-tasting leaf; used with lamb, pork, and veal roasts and roast chicken as well as in meatballs and soups.
mint	Available fresh or dried; used with cucumbers, in tabouli, cooked vegetables, and in summer vegetable soups and yogurt drinks as well as mint juleps; also as herbal tea or as a garnish.

mustard	Available as mustard seed or mustard powder, or in prepared mustard; used in salad dressings, marinades, and sauces as well as with meat, chicken, fish, vegetables, and cheese.
nutmeg	Available whole or powdered; essential to eggnog and very compatible with melted Swiss or Parmesan cheese, it lends flavor to cooked onions, mushrooms, potatoes, spinach, carrots, a variety of sauces, particularly white sauce, as well as cookies and cakes.
oregano	Actually a species of wild marjoram; much used in Spanish, Mexican, Italian, and Greek cooking; especially good in recipes containing tomatoes; also very compatible with cumin, basil, and rosemary.
paprika	A reddish-orange powder made from sweet red peppers; used in stews and sauces and with chicken to enrich both flavor and color, particularly in Hungarian cooking. Hungarian rose paprika is by far the best kind; other varieties are comparatively tasteless.
parsley	The most useful and available of all herbs. Use the leaves only unless you are blending or processing, in which case use both the leaves and the stems. A standard garnish, parsley is used in both cooked and uncooked dishes and is very dependable in revitalizing leftovers or helping soups and stews to realize their potential. Although curly parsley is more familiar than the Italian flat-leaf variety, the Italian has a more interesting taste.
peppercorns	References in this book are to black peppercorns, although white peppercorns

can be used when the uniform light color of a dish (a sauce, for example) seems threatened by black flecks. Green peppercorns, which can be bought in bottles, are suitable for pepper sauces (poivrades); red peppercorns, once much in vogue, are now viewed as possibly toxic. Black peppercorns can be crushed or ground; either way, they are at their best crushed or ground freshly at serving time.

pickling spices These are a blend of allspice, coriander, mustard seed, bay leaves, cloves, chilies, and pepper, used, as the name indicates, in making pickling solutions and also in boiling shellfish, meat, and vegetables. It is best to tie the spices in a square of cheesecloth bound with thread so that they can easily be removed at serving time.

poppy seeds These non-narcotic seeds of the poppy plant are used in baking, most interestingly as a filling called *mohn* in German and Jewish baking; the seeds are also excellent with noodles.

rosemary A very fragrant needle-like herb with a piney taste; excellent with lamb, pork, poultry, fish, and oranges. Best to crush the needles rather than use them whole.

sage Grayish green or bluish green leaves with a distinctive flavor traditionally used in stuffing chicken and turkey, as well as in sausage; an essential herb for Saltimbocca (page 49) and other Italian dishes.

savory Summer savory, an annual plant, has larger leaves than winter savory (a perennial) and is in greater supply. More delicate than winter savory, summer savory is particularly good with poultry, beef, lamb, and fish, and provides a refreshing flavor in salads, salad dressings, and bean soups as well as cooked vegetables.

sesame seeds The small flat seeds of the sesame plant lend flavor and texture sprinkled on rolls, bagels, or bread, or used as a coating for meat, poultry, or fish. The seeds are at their best lightly toasted in a moderate oven and are very good with vegetables and in omelets. They yield a delicious oil very suitable for sautéing and frying, and they are the main ingredient of *tahini*, the Middle Eastern counterpart of our peanut butter, a paste made with sesame seeds and often combined with chick-peas.

tarragon A tangy, anise-like flavor; used with fish and shellfish, chicken and veal, eggs, mushrooms, green vegetables (particularly artichokes), and tomatoes.

thyme Small gray-green leaves and a pleasant, pungent odor; used in stock, soups, stews, with roasted meats (especially good with lamb), fish and cooked vegetables.

Note: The French term *bouquet garni* referred to in this list is a collection of herbs—bay leaf, thyme, and parsley—held together in a small bundle, often tied in cheesecloth so that it can be easily removed before the dish is served. These herbs are the traditional seasoning for stock, soups, and stews.

Fines herbes is a mixture of chervil, tarragon, chives, and parsley—compatible herbs much favored for omelets and salad dressings. *Fines herbes* is a useful last-minute addition to any sauces and soups that seem to need "something more."

COMMERCIALLY PREPARED CONDIMENTS AND FLAVORINGS

almond extract	This is made from bitter almond oil. Be sure to buy the real thing—labeled "pure almond extract"—and not a synthetic preparation, which will only disappoint.
capers	These are the pickled buds and berries of a Mediterranean shrub; sold in bottles, they are sharp-tasting, salty, and very refreshing. They are especially effective in piquant sauces for meat, seafood, and eggs as well as salad dressings.
Dijon mustard	The term refers to a type of mustard, altogether different from American hot-dog mustard. Originally produced in Dijon, France, and now produced in the United States as well, Dijon mustard is made with white wine and spices and has a distinctive flavor. It can be spread on meat or fish; it can enhance egg salad, salad dressings, and sauces.
Louisiana hot sauce	This is made with aged red peppers and vinegar; it is not as strong as Tabasco sauce but still needs to be used with cau-

tion. Both sauces are much used in Creole or Cajun cooking.

Picante sauce

This is a Mexican hot sauce made with tomatoes, fresh peppers, onions, vinegar, salt, and spices. It is very zesty with eggs, meat, seafood, vegetables, soups, and salads, as well as tacos and enchiladas.

Soy, tamari, and teriyaki sauces

These Oriental sauces, made from fermented soybeans, are commonly used in stir-frying. They are very salty and should be avoided in low-sodium diets, though the imported sauces are less salty than the domestic.

Tabasco sauce

Made from Tabasco peppers, this is a powerful sauce and should be used with care in seasoning seafood, sauces, meat, soups, and eggs.

vanilla extract

This is made from vanilla beans and alcohol. As in the case of almond extract, look for the pure essence rather than any substitute.

Worcestershire sauce

This is a blending of vinegar, molasses, soy sauce, and anchovies that is used to flavor broiled meat, stews, soups, and piquant sauces.

BASIC FOODS TO KEEP ON HAND

This list contains enough to sustain life, enliven it from time to time, and come through for unexpected guests. Keep the following staples on hand, and of course supplement them with a continuous supply of fresh fruits and vegetables, milk, cheese, eggs, bread, fish, poultry, and meat.

The Pantry Shelf

Grains
Rice, barley, bulgur wheat, kasha, pasta and noodles, dried bean (a good variety including chick-peas), cornmeal, oatmeal, herbed bread crumbs.

Canned goods
Chicken and beef stock, canned tomatoes (preferably Italian plum tomatoes), tomato paste (try to find the kind in tubes—more expensive but once opened, it keeps much longer), tomato sauce, tomato juice or V-8, canned beans, chick-peas, water chestnuts, hearts of palm, hearts of artichoke, applesauce (in jars), pumpkin, pineapple (cubed, crushed, and sliced), plums, apricots; salmon, anchovies, shrimp, minced clams.

Miscellaneous
Potatoes, onions, honey, molasses, chocolate (bitter and semi-sweet), all-purpose flour, sugar (granulated, confectioners', and brown), baking powder, baking soda, pure vanilla ex-

tract, almond extract, cream of tartar, cooking oil (preferably unsaturated—safflower or corn oil), olive oil, wine vinegar, cider vinegar, peanut butter (preferably crunchy and not homogenized), bouillon cubes.

A selection of herbs and spices, including salt. (See the section: Herbs and Spices, page 246.)

And a selection from the following if you wish:
Cognac, Marsala, port, sherry, vermouth, red wine, white wine, rum, bourbon.

The Freezer

Nuts, Parmesan cheese, ginger root, pita or other bread, Italian sausage, bacon, enough recently purchased meat and chicken for at least a few meals, meat bones and chicken parts for stock, frozen peas, frozen spinach, pound cake, ice cream.

The Refrigerator

Dried fruit (raisins, currants, prunes, apricots, apples), coconut, marinated artichokes, canned lychees, eggs, cottage cheese, cream cheese, mayonnaise, butter or margarine, yogurt, cabbage, carrots.

Condiments for the refrigerator door:
Capers, Greek olives, Mexican picante sauce, Tabasco sauce, Worcestershire sauce, soy sauce, Dijon mustard, good sour pickles, little sweet pickles, preserves, jams, or jellies.

BASIC EQUIPMENT FOR YOUR KITCHEN

The following list is admittedly a compromise. There are cooks who love equipment—love hunting it down, taking it home, using it, taking care of it—in short, possessing it as fully as possible. There are also cooks who can make do with very little equipment and turn out remarkably good meals. The equipment suggested here is an ideal basic list, far from a bare minimum, but also far from an excessive amount.

For Preparing Foods

Blender and/or food processor
These are not exactly the same. A blender emulsifies liquids; a processor does not. And it is easier to blend soups and drinks in large quantity in a blender than a food processor. A processor can slice, chop, grate, and grind without the liquefying action of a blender. Both machines are useful in making purees. Processors are much cheaper than they once were; blenders are even cheaper. If you can buy both machines and keep them on the counter where you can use them readily, rather than in a cabinet, you will find you use them often.

In the absence of either of the above, an *electric mixer*, preferably a hand mixer that can be used at the stove, say, in beating an egg yolk in the top of a double boiler.

A *manual egg beater* or a *wire whisk* to take the place of an electric mixer.

set of stainless-steel *mixing bowls* of varying sizes

good-quality *knives* of several sizes, sharpened
   1 knife for cutting vegetables
   1 paring knife
   1 slicing knife for bread and meat
   1 small serrated knife for slicing lemons, tomatoes, and
     cucumbers
   1 small filleting knife for trimming the fat of meat

cutting board
spatula
soup ladle
3 large spoons:
   1 slotted metal spoon with a long handle
   1 metal kitchen spoon with a long handle
   1 wooden spoon for stirring grains to avoid scratching the
     saucepan; also for mixing batter

standard measuring cups and spoons
   transparent cup with a spout and measuring lines for
     liquids
   set of metal or plastic cups for measuring dry ingredients
   set of metal or plastic measuring spoons

pepper mill
potato ricer or masher
4-sided *grater*
salad dryer
colander
large strainer and *tea strainer*
orange juicer (manual or electric)
vegetable parer
garlic press
French-fry cutter
can opener
corkscrew
pair of *tongs*
vegetable brush
pastry brush
rubber or plastic spatula
aluminum foil
cheesecloth

For Stove-Top Cooking

Pots and pans
> 3 *covered saucepans* of varying sizes—4 quarts, 2 quarts, and 1 quart
> 1 *double boiler*

Saucepans and double boilers should have bottoms that will spread the heat evenly. Stainless-steel pots are tempting because they are easy to keep clean and shining and seem always to look new, but since stainless steel is a poor heat conductor, it needs to be combined with aluminum, which diffuses heat very well, or with copper, which conducts heat quickly. Either of these combinations, in a fairly heavy gauge, makes a serviceable utensil. Farberware, with aluminum sandwiched between layers of stainless steel, is very satisfactory. Aluminum by itself becomes pitted and discolored over the years, though it does the job of spreading heat evenly. People who care about the appearance of their kitchens seem to like copper: it is a beautiful material, but it is expensive and needs a good deal of attention and even repair (re-lining) from time to time.

2 *covered skillets*
One of these should be cast iron. It is inexpensive, conducts heat well, and is excellent for searing meats at high temperatures. In addition, it can be used in the oven or under the broiler, as skillets with wooden or Bakelite handles cannot. A 9½-inch size is very useful. (If you have many guests, you may also want the 12$\frac{7}{16}$ size.) Just be sure you follow the manufacturer's directions for seasoning the pan before you use it. Always dry it, and never use scouring powder.

You will also need a small skillet, say, a stainless steel or enamel 7½-inch size, or a treated no-stick pan.

small collapsible *vegetable steamer* to fit most saucepans

potato baker
This dome-shaped metal cover over a round metal rack is an inexpensive and extremely useful gadget in all seasons. In

warm weather it permits you to bake potatoes or acorn squash on the stove, without lighting the oven. (If you rush to your potato baker when you first come home after work and scrub a good-sized potato for each person, you will have the dinner started and perhaps you can relax, knowing you have before you a legitimate baked potato—nothing like the gray, re-heated and tasteless version offered by so many restaurants that try to disguise its bleakness with aluminum foil and too much sour cream.)

large *covered crock* or large covered glass or ceramic casserole for marinating meat.

For Baking and Broiling

broiling pan with a rack to fit
Ovenproof baking dishes in several sizes for casseroles
1 or 2 *cookie sheets*
1 or 2 *bread pans*
muffin tins for a dozen muffins
2 *baking pans*
   8- or 9-inch-square pan
   oblong ceramic 9- by 12-inch pan for baking cakes (or roasting meat)
2 *round cake pans*
custard cups
8- *or 9-inch pie plate*
soufflé dish or straight-sided round and deep oven dish
8- or 10-inch *quiche pan*
bean pot
rolling pin
bulb baster
small *gratin dishes*
skewers for shish kebab
thermometers
   meat thermometer
   oven thermometer
   candy thermometer

For Storing

1 or 2 Corning Ware pots for freezing, storing in the refrigerator, and baking (but not usually recommended for cooking)

Mason jars for storing grains

jars of various sizes—large enough for transferring a tall can of tomato juice, small enough for leftovers and the unused contents of cans

airtight container for cheese straws, certain kinds of cookies, etc.

For Serving

several attractive bowls and platters in various sizes

several large serving spoons

meat fork

salad bowl—preferably glass or ceramic and large enough for tossing greens with dressing

salad fork and spoon

Optional Equipment

mortar and pestle
crockpot
wok
deep fryer
small chafing dish
large chafing dish
meat grinder
ice cream scoop
coffee mill

Other Useful Items

pot holders

tea towels

tiles or trivets or straw mats for hot oven dishes brought to
the table

apron to cover you as completely as possible

roll of cash register tape mounted on the kitchen wall (in a
wooden frame or any other arrangement): to be used
only for shopping lists

telephone cord long enough to permit you to reach the stove,
sink, or refrigerator if you must when you're impaled by
a telephone caller in the middle of cooking

box of baking soda near the stove to put out grease fires

aloe plant on the windowsill in case of burns

HINTS, SUGGESTIONS, AND SHORTCUTS

Some General Advice in the Kitchen

To avoid accidents at the stove, do not wear long billowy sleeves when you cook. Wipe the bottom of the skillet with paper towels after pouring out bacon fat or other grease; in any event, never place a skillet with a greasy bottom over the gas or electric unit. It is wise to keep a box of baking soda within easy reach to put out grease fires.

Keep pot handles from projecting off the stove. And check *frequently* on what's cooking and how it's doing—except when you're steaming rice. Rice should not be disturbed.

If you have an electric stove, be aware that the heat doesn't cut back as fast as it does in a gas stove. To avoid burning food, remove the pot or pan for a half-minute or so until the heat is reduced, and then proceed.

Check the temperature setting of your oven against an oven thermometer to make sure they coincide. If they don't, be guided by the oven thermometer, particularly if you plan to bake.

To boil water quickly, cover the pot.

Keep your kitchen knives sharp. There are few things as dispiriting as trying to cut with a knife that won't do its job.

To heat platters and dinner dishes, use an oven that has been heated (low or medium) and then turned off. Some people use the drying cycle of their dishwashers to heat dishes before serving; others simply run hot water over them and then dry them off.

To clean scorched pans, add ¼ cup of baking soda to ½ cup of water, boil 5 to 10 minutes, and the burned material will loosen.

To crack rather than grind fresh pepper, loosen the tension in your pepper mill.

To keep salt flowing freely in humid weather, place a few grains of uncooked rice in the saltcellar.

To avoid overloading your blender, combine ingredients in two stages until you get a good sense of the capacity of your machine.

Pointers on Shopping and Storing

Always have a list with you when you shop. If you shop when you're hungry, you will, the psychologists warn us, buy impulsively.

Don't overbuy fresh fruit and vegetables or they will lose their bloom before you get around to eating them.

When you buy a container of yogurt, cottage cheese, or sour cream, check the top to see if it has already been opened and then put back by another customer.

In buying eggs, always open the box and check for cracked or broken eggs.

Try to notice the expiration dates on perishable products.

Avoid buying swollen cans because of the danger of botulism.

To buy ground beef with the smallest amount of fat, choose a package of lean stewing beef and ask the butcher to grind it for you. If you buy several packages at once, ask him to wrap the meat in as many small packages as you wish. Freeze what you don't use immediately; it will keep for several months in the freezer (but no more than two days in the refrigerator).

In the supermarket never hesitate to ring the butcher's bell —once you've found it—and ask for his help.

Never store leftover canned food (particularly tomato products) in the can; transfer the contents to a jar or some other container. If you're short of containers, use empty yogurt or cottage cheese containers, making sure they are well washed. They can be used in the freezer as well as the refrigerator.

Rather than leave unused grains in an opened box, transfer them to jars with tight-fitting lids. Be sure to cut out the cooking instructions on the box and tape them to the jar.

After you've opened a bag of pretzels, potato chips, cookies, etc., slip the opened package into a plastic bag and tie it well, so that the contents will stay fresh.

In the summer, keep canned salmon, shrimp, and juices in the refrigerator so that they will be well chilled when you want them.

Keep small quantities of leftover food in the freezer for use in soups later on. Be sure to wrap leftovers well in aluminum foil or put them in a covered plastic container with a clearly written label.

Poultry and Meat

In preparing poultry, remove the package (or packages) of viscera from the cavity. Rinse and freeze the gizzard and heart for future chicken soup; rinse and freeze the liver separately for a future chicken liver dish.

Rinse the cavity under cold running water, removing as much of the fat surrounding the opening as possible. Pat dry with paper towels.

It's best to remove poultry, meat, or fish from the refrigerator at least half an hour before placing it in the oven. (At the refrigerated temperature, the outside will cook much faster than the inside in a heated oven.)

For the sake of your health, remove as much visible fat from the meat as you can, and be sure you cut away any meat stamped with the blue dye of the meat inspectors.

If you cut stewing beef into small pieces (that is, cut each of the butcher's chunks into quarters), the stew will have a good deal more flavor: the more surface, the better the flavor.

To slice raw meat easily, freeze it for an hour before slicing.

To roast meat, place it on a rack that fits the oven pan so that the bottom of the meat will not be cooked too fast by the fat that drips down. Also, pour a thin layer of water under the rack to keep the pan from burning.

After removing roasted meat or poultry from the oven, let it rest 15 minutes before carving it so that the juices don't rush out when the first slice is cut. You can keep the roast warm by placing it on the oven door after turning off the oven.

When you bring a roasted chicken or duck or turkey to the table and begin to carve, only to find the bird is undercooked, remove the platter with a flourish, complete the carving in the kitchen, and place the slices in the broiler pan. Broil watchfully, spooning the roasting pan juices over the meat to keep it moist.

Eggs

If it's at all possible, take the eggs out of the refrigerator for an hour or two before cooking them. They cook best at room temperature.

To test eggs for freshness cover them with cold salted water; fresh eggs will stay at the bottom. Don't use any eggs that bob to the top.

In preparing eggs for omelets, scrambled eggs, or frittata, don't overbeat; the resulting foam may burn.

If you hard-cook eggs for future use and refrigerate them, mark them with a pencil so that you won't confuse them with raw eggs.

Fruits and Vegetables

To ripen apricots, nectarines, peaches, plums, and pears, place them in a paper bag and close it loosely.

If you buy green bananas, leave them at room temperature until they are yellow. If they become speckled, put them in the refrigerator—contrary to conventional wisdom; they will keep there for as long as a week. Even if they turn blackish, don't throw them away: peel them, wrap them in foil, and freeze them for use in blended drinks.

Store melons at room temperature until they are ripe (or really smell like melons).

Wash strawberries (and other berries) just before you use them, no earlier.

To peel the skin of citrus fruits as a flavoring agent, use a potato parer or a sharp knife and cut away only the colored part of the skin (called the zest); the white is bitter.

For more juice, roll citrus fruits against a table or counter before juicing.

Sprinkle freshly peeled fruits with lemon juice to prevent discoloration.

Store tomatoes at room temperature and away from direct sunlight until they are ripe; then put them in the refrigerator.

If carrots or celery go limp, put them in a container with water and ice cubes, or put them in the refrigerator for a few hours in a container of water. (Keep a fresh supply of crisp carrots and celery for hungry children—and adults—to stave off junk food binges if dinner is delayed.)

Keep bean sprouts and bean curd (tofu) in a bowl of water in the refrigerator and be sure to change the water every day.

Heat changes green vegetables very rapidly. Unless you keep an eye on them while they cook, they can easily turn to mush. Respect their color and texture and serve them before they lose either.

If you boil green vegetables (rather than steam them), leave the lid off or the water will become too hot to preserve the color and taste.

To draw off some of the bitter liquid in eggplant, prepare it in this way before sautéing or frying: remove the stems, wash, and slice into rounds (¼ to ⅜ inch thick). Lay the slices on paper towels and sprinkle heavily with salt. Ten minutes later, turn the slices and repeat the salt treatment. Rinse under cold tap water and dry with paper towels before frying in hot fat.

To avoid the smell that accompanies the cooking of Brussels sprouts, cabbage, broccoli, or leeks, wrap a piece of bread in cheesecloth and place it in the water or the steaming basket.

Use a vegetable brush to scrub the skins of vegetables if you don't wish to pare them. Retaining the skins means retaining valuable minerals.

Sautéing and Frying

Sautéing should be done quickly over high or medium-high heat.

Because butter tends to burn over high heat, if you want a buttery flavor when sautéing, add unmelted butter to hot oil.

In frying, be sure the food is absolutely dry before it is put into hot oil. Otherwise the moisture will cause spattering and the food will not fry properly.

Be sure the food to be fried is ready to be cooked at the moment the oil is hot enough: don't try to prepare it while the oil is heating.

Drop only small quantities at a time into the hot oil so that you don't cause a sudden drop in temperature.

Drain fried foods on paper towels and then place in a dish in an open, heated oven until serving time.

Baking

Insert a sharp knife in the center of a cake or pie to determine when it is done. The knife should come out relatively dry.

If the top of a pie or cake seems to be browning too quickly and you have reason to think the center is not done, cover the top with aluminum foil.

When you bake cookies, remove them from the cookie sheet

with a spatula when they are done and transfer them to a rack to cool.

To cut a cake into two or more layers, use a thread or a length of dental floss rather than a knife, holding the thread or floss by both ends and guiding it steadily through the cake.

Correcting Oversalting

To correct dishes that have been oversalted, drop a halved raw potato into the soup or stew you think you have ruined. Let the potato cook as long as possible and remove it before serving the dish. If the dish is still salty, a tablespoon of cream or unsalted butter may help.

To reduce the amount of salt in canned vegetables (should you absolutely need to use them), drain and rinse them for 1 minute under plain tap water.

Rinsing tuna fish for 3 minutes under tap water will remove most of the salt.

Dealing with Onions

If you really detest peeling and cutting onions, or if you have no time to do it, substitute scallions wherever possible, or use bulb onions when they are available.

If you need to peel a great many onions, plunge them into boiling water and count 10 slowly; then transfer them to cold water and count again. The skins should slip off easily by then. Cut off the root end last.

To cut an onion without tears, place it in the freezer for an hour, or peel it under cold running water. If you plan to sauté or fry the onion, dry it with paper towels before chopping.

To slice an onion easily, cut it in half, place both halves on a cutting board flat side down, and slice with a sharp knife.

Store a cut onion in a covered jar in the refrigerator.

To get rid of the odor, after peeling and cutting onions (or garlic) wash your hands with baking soda.

Improvisations

To make buttermilk when you have none on hand, mix ½ teaspoon of white vinegar with ¼ cup of milk.

Crème fraîche, the thick, delicious French cream now much in demand, is an excellent alternative to our whipped cream, and many people feel it is superior both in flavor and dependability. Because it has matured, it will not curdle when boiled, and it will last about 2 weeks refrigerated. To make your own version combine 1 cup of heavy cream and 2 tablespoons of buttermilk in a jar with a screw top. Cover and shake well (2 to 3 minutes); let the mixture stand unrefrigerated overnight until the cream seems thick. Then refrigerate.

Dieters: As a salad dressing, try pulverizing a fresh tomato in your blender or processor, seasoning it with a pinch of basil or dill. Pickle juice is another possibility instead of an oil-based dressing.

For quick pasta, use the tiniest kind, which cooks in 5 to 6 minutes: acini di pepe or rosamarina. Add butter and Parmesan cheese and toss well. And if you are an Oriental food fan, substitute Oriental cellophane noodles for the pasta.

If you're pressed for time and can't produce a homemade dessert, aside from the obvious solution of going to a good bakery, consider serving cheese and fruit: for example, Brie or Camembert with seedless grapes; Stilton, Gorgonzola, or Roquefort with peaches, plums, or wedges of ripe pear; Provolone, Gruyère, or Vermont Cheddar with wedges of Granny Smith apples; or any cream cheese-like cheese with strawberries or apricots. Serve the cheese at room temperature and sprinkle any cut fruit with a few drops of lemon juice.

What to Do with Leftovers

Leftovers are almost inevitable. One way to deal with them is simply to throw them out, and some people do. Others, with tenderer consciences, have the support of a long tradition of French cooking that is based solidly on the idea of conserving what is valuable. It takes some thought and a little practice to use leftovers well, but conversely, they can trigger the imagination in all sorts of ways.

I suggest that busy people *plan* to use leftovers. Doubling the amount of rice, pasta, bulgur wheat, beans, or other vegetables will give you something already cooked for the next meal. Any of these can be metamorphosed into a salad (see, for example, Pasta Salad, page 171 or Bulgur Wheat Salad, page 170). Cooked rice can also be used in fried rice, Beef and Brown Rice (page 71), or Respectably Refurbished Leftover Rice (page 195). Cooked potatoes can be revived, as in Simple Potato Soufflé (page 152). Baked sweet potatoes keep perfectly without any loss of flavor; so you can bake enough for two nights.

Since stews are even better the second night, consider tripling the recipe for beef stew and serving it on night one, night two, and again later in the week (to give yourself a reprieve).

If you embark on a roast to see you through the week (as many people do), you may want cold slices and something hot to accompany them, unless it's summer, when a completely cold meal is welcome. If you have leftover beef, use it in Fleischsalat (page 168). If, however, you wish to reheat the meat, use a double boiler. Place the slices of meat with some of its gravy in the top of a double boiler. If there is no gravy left, use 1 tablespoon of butter and 3 tablespoons of water. Cover and bring the water to a boil. Then turn the heat off so that the meat is warmed as gently as possible to preserve its texture. Better yet, make an onion sauce (page 177) and place the meat in it: the meat will be wonderfully revived.

For small, problematic amounts of leftovers, a good friend

of mine makes a very acceptable diet soup in a blender, using 1 cup of cooked vegetables, 1 cup of the water in which they were cooked (save that too—in a covered jar), 1 bouillon cube, and 1 cup of skim milk (you can use whole milk if you prefer). She adds some spices, always varying the seasoning to suit the particular vegetable, and blends it all together. Feeling triply virtuous because she has used leftovers and produced a low-calorie and low-cholesterol soup, she serves it either chilled or hot, depending on the season. With broccoli, she likes nutmeg; with cabbage, a fresh scallion and a fresh tomato. I have used her basic recipe, using 1 cup of zucchini and 2 tablespoons of Chinese preserved onions (see page 44), ½ cup of cottage cheese, ¾ cup of milk, a few drops of bottled Mexican picante sauce, and a pinch of dillweed.

If invention fails and you simply want to reheat what you have on hand without any variations, place the leftovers in the top of a double boiler or in a slow oven in a covered oven dish, being sure to add a little stock, tomato juice, or gravy.

What to do if all you have in the refrigerator is a little cottage cheese or hard cheese and some leftover vegetables? Bake them together with a few herbs, or sauté the vegetables in a pan, add the cheese, and stir from time to time. Cover for a few minutes at the end, until the cheese melts.

Consider using very small amounts of leftovers as fillings in frittata or a soufflé-omelet (see the section on eggs, page 107).

USEFUL TECHNIQUES

A good many basic procedures are explained in the recipes themselves. The following have been referred to but not explained.

How to measure

To measure liquids, use a clear glass measuring cup and be sure that your eye is on a level with the line marking the amount you need. To measure dry ingredients, use a set of plastic or metal cups (1 cup, ½ cup, ⅓ cup, ¼ cup) and be sure to choose the right one. Fill the measure loosely (except when the recipe calls for tight packing, as with brown sugar). Fill the cup to the top and run a table knife across the surface to make it level.

To measure dry ingredients with measuring spoons, use a knife in the same way, leveling off the surface.

How to whip cream

Be sure to use heavy (whipping) cream. When the cream has begun to thicken, add vanilla, sugar, or other flavorings should you want them. *With a wire whisk or eggbeater (manual or electric)*: Chill the whisk or eggbeater. Chill a metal bowl (in hot weather, set it in a pan of ice cubes). Beat until the cream thickens. If you have overbeaten and the cream is on its way to becoming butter, add 2 to 3 tablespoons of cold milk and whip briefly.

In the blender: Chill the blender jar and be sure it is clean and perfectly dry. Pour the heavy cream into the jar. Cover and switch the machine on and off at high speed once a second for 10 seconds. Remove the lid, check to see if the cream is thick enough, and if it is not, flick the switch two or three more times. Be careful not to overblend.

In the food processor: Chill the workbowl and the blade. Process the cream for 1 minute, check to see whether it is thick enough, and continue processing a few more seconds— until you see a rim forming on the workbowl.

How to separate egg whites from egg yolks

First check the freshness of the eggs (see freshness test, page 266).

Some cooks pour the yolk from one half of the broken shell to another, letting the egg whites fall into a bowl. Others, less squeamish, slide the contents of the egg shell into the cup of one hand, letting the whites run out between the fingers into a bowl. I recommend the first method. There are also commercial devices to separate eggs.

How to beat egg whites

No matter what method you use in separating, if there is any trace of egg yolk in the white, you will not succeed in beating the white properly. If you cannot fish out the bit of yolk with a clean half-shell, abandon the attempt; save the white for another dish such as tomorrow's scrambled eggs or place it in the freezer in a small container. Start again.

On the other hand, a little egg white mixed in the yolk will not really matter. For this reason, if the recipe calls for beating both parts of the egg, beat the whites first, and you won't have to wash and dry the beater and the bowl when you beat the yolks. Just remember: the whites will not tolerate foreign matter. The beater and the bowl must be perfectly clean and dry.

With a wire whisk or egg beater (manual or electric): As you beat, keep pushing the whites down with a rubber spatula as they climb the sides of the bowl. Turn the bowl and move the position of the beaters in the bowl to incorporate all of the white. When the whites are frothy, add cream of tartar (¼ teaspoon for 4 egg whites) or salt or sugar, as the recipe directs. Continue beating to the desired degree of stiffness.

In the blender: Pour the egg whites into the blender jar and cover. Blend until the whites are frothy, then add the cream of tartar, etc. Blend a few seconds more for stiffly beaten whites or whites that form peaks.

In the food processor: With this method you must use at least 4 egg whites to succeed. Add the cream of tartar or salt to the whites and then process until peaks form.

Note: Do not attempt to use either the blender or the processor for folding. Transfer the whites to a bowl and fold by the rule below.

How to beat egg yolks

When the directions call for beating the yolks until they are pale creamy-yellow or thick and lemon-colored, beat them until you can drop a little from the egg beater or wire whisk back into the bowl. You should then see something like a ribbon settling itself when it is dropped.

How to fold

The heavier ingredients should always be below the lighter: therefore, you should mix the lighter into the heavier, not the other way around. Folding refers to the process of blending a foamy or fragile mixture into a heavier one without deflating the foam. To do this, rotate the bowl with the one hand and use the other to insert a rubber spatula straight down through the middle of the bowl, scraping the bottom and bringing the spatula up to the top. Work as quickly and deftly as you can, to lose as little air as possible.

How to make hard-cooked eggs

For 4 large eggs, bring 1 quart of water to a boil in a saucepan. With a pin, pierce the large end of the egg to allow the air trapped inside the shell to escape. Using a slotted spoon, gently lower the eggs into the boiling water. Add 1½ teaspoons of salt. Lower the heat and boil gently for 12 minutes.

Drain the eggs, and either cover them with cold water for a few minutes, or, to help ensure neat peeling, refrigerate them for a couple of hours. Crack the shells gently all over. Holding each egg under running water, remove its membrane and shell, starting from the large end of the egg.

How to toast nuts and seeds

Place them on a cookie sheet and bake them in a medium (300°) oven for 8 to 10 minutes. Cool.

How to peel garlic easily

Drop the clove in boiling water for half a minute, allow to cool, and slip the skin off with your fingers.

How to make chicken stock

Use your freezer to store the gizzards, hearts, necks, and backs of successive chickens plus any leftover bits you may have from fairly recently cooked chickens. Keep all this in a freezer container plainly marked *Chicken Stock*. When you have enough to bother with (i.e., what feels like 2 pounds or so), put them all together in 5 to 6 cups of water. Wash a carrot and add it to the pot; add a peeled onion, a peeled clove of garlic, and a *bouquet garni* (see page 252). Bring to a boil, then lower the heat and simmer 2 hours. Correct the seasoning. Strain through a colander, ideally one lined with cheesecloth, and allow the stock to cool. Refrigerate and then remove the layer of fat that comes to the top during refrigeration. To store for more than 3 days, place in the freezer. You may want to divide the stock into small containers before freezing.

If you do all this, you will have a quantity of rather priceless liquid. There is nothing I know of sold commercially that is comparable: not canned soup, which is over-salted and full of preservatives; not bouillon cubes, which taste like bouillon cubes, not chicken soup. One wonders that so useful and lovable a commodity has not been marketed in a satisfactory way.

A second method, used in family cooking in France and elsewhere, is to put a chicken carcass* and some of the gravy into a pot of cold water, adding the vegetables and seasonings listed above. Boil for an hour, correct the seasoning, strain, refrigerate, and remove the fat.

How to make beef stock

Proceed as with chicken stock, using a few pounds of beef bones that have been stored in the freezer. (Use both bones from the butcher and leftover cooked bones.) Place them in a large enough pot, cover with water, and flavor with the vegetables and seasonings suggested for chicken stock. Follow through to the final step in which the surface fat is removed after refrigeration; then divide into smaller quantities, if you wish, and store in the freezer.

How to prepare dried beans

Beans are a low-fat, cholesterol-free source of protein, rich in vitamins, minerals, and dietary fiber, and deserving of greater popularity. The variety is wonderful: there are white beans, black beans, red beans, pintos, kidney beans, limas, lentils, chick-peas—and others. The easiest way to use them is, of course, to open a can and rinse them in a colander. If, however, you wish to avoid the additives used in canned beans or if you are cooking in quantity, use dried beans, which are very inexpensive and simple to cook. Once you cook them, if you are not planning to use them all at once, divide them into as many small portions as you wish, storing each in a freezer container. Label and freeze.

* The carcass from the Chicken with Garlic recipe (see page 81) makes first-rate stock.

1. Spread the beans out in a large platter and pick out any pebbles or foreign matter. Rinse in a colander under cold running water and place in a large pot to soak overnight. Use 1 quart of water for every cup of dried beans.

2. In the morning, drain the beans and fill the pot with fresh water. Bring it to a rapid boil, reduce the heat, and simmer for 1 hour, uncovered.

3. Test the beans for doneness and salt to taste. Drain and use as the recipe directs.

Note: As an alternative to the overnight soaking method, using the same proportion of water to beans (1 quart water to 1 cup dried beans), bring the water to a rolling boil, add the beans, and when the water returns to a boil, cook the beans 3 minutes. Remove from the heat and cover, letting the beans swell for 1 hour. Return the pot to the heat and simmer, uncovered, for 1½ hours.

To make the beans more digestible:

1. Soak the beans for 4 hours and discard the water.

2. Start again with cold water—same proportions—this time bringing the water to a boil and cooking the beans for 30 minutes. Drain them again and discard the water.

3. Repeat Step 2. Test the beans for doneness. They should be thoroughly cooked; cook a little longer if they are not.

GLOSSARY OF COOKING TERMS

Al dente: literally, "to the tooth"—an Italian phrase that describes pasta at its best, when it is firm and chewy and not overcooked.

Baste: to spoon the pan juices over roasting meat; often done with a bulb baster.

Blanch: to drop food into boiling water for a short time in order to tame the taste of vegetables like broccoli or onions, or soften the texture; also used to remove the skins of tomatoes, peaches, or almonds. (Almonds, for example, should be blanched for half a minute, then cooled, and the skins will slip off. Tomatoes and peaches take about 10 seconds.)

Boil: to heat liquid until the surface erupts in large bubbles. To make tea, always bring the water to an unmistakable boil, a "rolling" boil. When you are asked to "bring to a boil, reduce the heat, and simmer," either remove the food from the heat for a few seconds or add cold water by the spoon.

Caramelize: to heat sugar slowly until syrupy and light brown, or to cook foods like fruit or nuts in such a syrup until light brown.

Clarify: to melt butter, retaining only the clear yellow portion and removing and discarding the milky residue. (See page 236.)

Cream: to beat shortening, or shortening and sugar, until creamy in texture.

Cube: to cut into pieces the shape of cubes.

Deep-fry: to cook in hot fat that completely covers the food.

Deglaze: to add liquid (water, stock, or wine) to a pan in which meat has cooked and use it to dissolve any remaining small particles of the meat and its juices.

Dice: to cut food into very small cubes.

Dot: to place tiny amounts over the surface of a dish, as, for example, to dot with butter.

Dust: to sprinkle with flour or sugar. To dust cakes with confectioners' sugar, press the sugar with the back of a large spoon through a strainer, covering the surface evenly. To dust cookies on both sides, cover a large plate with a layer of strained sugar, place the cookies over it, and strain more sugar over the surface of the cookies.

Fold: to incorporate a light mixture carefully into a heavy one (see page 275).

Fry: see *Deep-fry* and *Sauté*.

Glaze: to coat by caramelizing (*see* Caramelize, above), or to strain and boil fruit preserves until slightly stiff for icing on a cake; also to baste roasted meats with a sweet liquid that will create a glazed surface.

Gratiné: to produce a golden brown surface under the broiler, often by means of butter, bread crumbs, or grated cheese, or a combination. *Au gratin* refers to the crust produced in this way.

Mince: to chop into fine pieces.

Parboil: to cook only partway by boiling; the assumption is that a further cooking step is to follow.

Puree: to rub through a strainer, or to mash until the food is in a semisolid state; a puree can also be made in a blender or processor.

Reduce: to boil down a sauce to intensify its flavor and thicken it.

Roux: a mixture of hot fat and flour used as the base for white or brown sauce.

Sauté: to cook in a small amount of hot fat.

Score: to cut the surface of meat in a pattern, as, for example, a ham, which is often scored in diamond shapes before being glazed.

Sear: to brown the surface of meat quickly on high heat so that the juices do not run out.

Simmer: to cook in liquid gently, just below the boiling point.

Steam: as the term is used in this book, to cook in the steam of boiling water by placing food in a sievelike container just above the level of the water; the pot should be covered.

Zest: the colored part of the skin of citrus fruits, used for flavoring. The white part is bitter; only the zest should be used.

SAMPLE MENUS

Brunch

Choose any one from each of the following groups:

Broiled Grapefruit (page 30)
Instant Fresh Applesauce (page 203)
Frozen Grapes and Yogurt (page 205)
Fresh fruit juice or tomato juice
Fresh ripe fruit—honeydew, cantaloupe,
apricots, peaches, or plums

Eggs with Ham or Asparagus in Cheese Sauce (page 110)
Spinach Timbale (page 118)
Scrambled Eggs and Smoked Salmon (page 115)
Frittata with Vegetables (page 108)
Cottage Cheese Pancakes (page 117)
Welsh Rarebit (page 113)
Ricotta Pie (page 111)

Appalachian Corn Bread (page 201)
Irish Soda Bread (page 202) with butter and marmalade
Fried Bread (page 198)

Hot rolls, bagels, pita, sourdough rye or French bread
and, if you wish, one of the following:

Berliner Brot (page 238)
Homemade Granola Fruit Bars (page 235)
A sweet bread (pumpkin, zucchini, cranberry,
orange-date, etc.)

Coffee or Tea

Lunch

Avocado Soup (page 46)
Corned Beef and Pickle Salad (page 161)
with toasted rye bread
Cherry tomatoes
Sour Apple Pie (page 232)

Chilled steamed green beans
with Basic Salad Dressing (page 173)
Grilled Fish with Mustard (page 100)
New Potatoes (page 138)
Lychees and Yogurt (page 208)

Cock-a-Leekie Soup (page 43)
Eggs in Burgundy (page 114)
Crusty French bread or Mashed Potatoes (page 137)
Lettuce Salad with Basic Salad Dressing (page 173)
Cheese and fresh fruit

White Bean Salad (page 156)
Chicken Livers with Artichoke Hearts (page 91)
Elevated Applesauce (page 204)
Greek Shortbread (page 236)

Black Bean Soup (page 44)
Appalachian Corn Bread (page 201)
Ham and Melon Salad (page 162)
Ice Cream with Bitter Chocolate Sauce (page 221)

Picnic Lunches

Cold Cucumber Soup (page 38)
Shish Kebab (page 61)
Rice Pilaf (page 194)
Strawberry Pie (page 234)

Simple Salmon Timbale (page 105)
Cold chicken (from any of the chicken recipes)
Roman Potato Salad (page 164)
Carrot sticks
Fresh fruit in season
Homemade Granola Fruit Bars (page 235)

Smoked Fish Salad (page 169)
Ham Sandwiches (slices from Baked Ham, page 53)
Onion Tart (page 149) or Ricotta Pie (page 111)
Fresh fruit in season
Tipsy Pudding (page 231)

8 Small Dinner Parties

Winter Menus

Cabbage Soup (page 36)

Chicken with Sausage (page 87)
Polenta (page 197)
Green and Red Roasted Peppers (page 136)

Glazed Pears (page 210)

Cold Marinated Leeks (page 133)

Galotsie Polonaise (page 244)
Potatoes with Horseradish and Mustard Sauce (page 179)

Cranberry-Raspberry Ice Cream (page 216)

Curried Spinach Soup (page 35)

Beef Stew and Tea-Soaked Raisins (page 74)
Rice Pilaf (page 194)
Grated Sautéed Zucchini (page 144)

Oranges in Wine (page 207)

Onion Soup (page 36)

Lemon Chicken (page 86)
Buttered noodles
Glazed Carrots (page 127)

Coconut Pie (page 233)

Summer Menus

Pasta Salad (page 171)

Saltimbocca (page 49)
Broccoli with Garlic and Nuts (page 124)

Zabaglione (page 211)

Ham and Melon Salad (page 162)

Chicken Breast with Hearts of Palm (page 85)
New Potatoes (page 138)
Green salad with Basic Salad Dressing (page 173)

Frozen Berry Cream (page 217)

Chilled Beet Soup (page 37)

Shrimp in Beer (page 99)
Fried Bread (page 198)
Spinach salad with Salsa Verde (page 178)

Bløtkake (page 225)

Blender Plum Soup (page 45)

Fresh Trout (page 103)
Sautéed Red Radishes (page 142)
Rice Pilaf (page 194)

Forgotten Torte (page 224)
filled with Mocha Mousse (page 218)

5 Meatless Dinners

Fresh Melon

Baked Fish Fillets with Mushrooms (page 101)
"Crispy and Delicious" Green Beans (page 131)
Simple Potato Soufflé (page 152)

Pears with Cointreau (page 228)

Tabouli (page 170)

Baked Soufflé-Omelet with Mushrooms and
Feta Cheese (page 116)
Leeks Rissolés (page 132)

Pound cake and Bitter Chocolate Sauce (page 221)

Baba Ghanouj (page 27)

Falafel Cake (page 146) with yogurt and chopped
tomatoes and cucumbers

Fresh fruit in season

Fried Cheese, or Saganaki (page 112)

A vegetable platter: Fresh Beets with Dill (page 123)
Braised Celery (page 128)
Fried Green Tomatoes (page 143)

Creamy Rice Pudding (page 212)

Egg Salad (page 160) served on a bed of
shredded romaine lettuce

Green Peas in the Lebanese Manner (page 150)
with feta cheese or bean curd and brown rice

Chocolate Ricotta Frozen Dessert (page 219)

3 Dinners for Unexpected Guests

Emergency Tomato Soup (page 40)
Beef with Bulgur Wheat (page 68)
Celery and carrot sticks
Glazed Bananas (page 206)

Hard-Cooked Eggs with Mayonnaise (page 29)
Pasta with Clam Sauce (page 183)
Green salad with Parmesan or
Blue Cheese Dressing (page 173)
Iced Coffee with Ice Cream (page 220)

Cucumber Salad (page 158)
Hamburger Pie (page 75)
Barley Pilaf (page 194)
Instant Fresh Applesauce (page 203)

A Holiday Dinner

Scallops in the Shell (page 97)
Roast Duckling (page 95)
Mashed Potatoes (page 137) with nutmeg
Baked Onions (page 134)
Mixed green salad with Basic Salad Dressing with
Dijon Mustard (page 173)
Fresh Cranberry Relish (page 192)
Chocolate Cups (page 223) filled with ice cream

A Buffet Dinner Party

Baked Ham (page 53)
Baked Beans (page 241)
Coleslaw (page 166)
Irish Soda Bread (page 202)
Pineapple Sherbet (page 229)

A Cocktail Party

Toasted Almonds
Baba Ghanouj (page 27) with small pita wedges
Baked Mushrooms (page 28)
Caviar Spread (page 26) with thin pumpernickel
Marinated mixed vegetables—green peppers, cauliflower,
Brussels Sprouts (page 133)
Carrot and celery sticks
Cherry tomatoes
Cheese Straws (page 239)

A Wedding Buffet

Champagne punch
Open Shrimp Sandwiches (page 31)
Smoked Fish Salad (page 169)
Corned Beef and Pickle Salad (page 161)
Grape and Watercress Salad (page 159)
Wedding "Pie" (page 242)
Bløtkake (page 225)

INDEX

Dicing, 280
Diet recipes
  blender diet soup, 271
  Broiled Grapefruit, 30
  Broiled Potatoes, 141
  Buffalo Chicken Wings, 90
  Cabbage Soup or Onion Soup,
    36
  Chocolate Ricotta Frozen
    Dessert, 219
  Cold Cucumber Soup, 38
  Dieter's Mushroom Soup, 39
  Easy Oven-Fried Chicken, 84
  Egg and Lemon Soup, 42
  Egg Noodles, 196
  Emergency Tomato Soup, 40
  Falafel Cake, 146
  Pineapple Sherbet, 229
  salad dressing, 270
  substitutions for rich foods, 17
  White Sauce, 180
  Yorkshire Pudding, 199
  See also Fish and Shellfish,
    Poultry, Salads, Vegetables
Dinners that cook themselves
  A Feast from the Oven, 243
  Galotsie Polonaise, 244
  Stewed Chicken with Beer and
    Olives, 94
  See also Stews
Dips
  Anchovy Sauce, 176
  Caviar Spread, 26
  Eggplant Salad, 27
  Shrimp Spread, 23
Dotting, 280
Dressings for salad
  basic, for green salad, 173
  blue cheese, 174
  for Coleslaw or Carrot Salad,
    175
  for dieters, 270
  for fruit salad, 174
Dried apples (schnitz), 232
Duck
  Roast Duckling, 95
Dusting, 280

Egg whites, beating, 274
Eggplant
  Baked Eggplant, 130
  Chicken Breast and Eggplant,
    93
  drawing off bitterness in, 267
  Eggplant Salad (Baba
    Ghanouj), 27
  steaming, 130
Eggs
  Baked Soufflé-Omelet, 116
  beating, 266, 274–75
  boiling, 276
  Camper's Meal-in-One, 119
  Egg and Lemon Soup
    (Avgolemono), 42
  Egg Salad, 160
    in Wedding "Pie," 242
  Eggs in Burgundy, 114
  Eggs Kiev, 240
  Eggs with Ham or Asparagus
    in Cheese Sauce, 110
  Frittata, 108
  Hard-Cooked Eggs with
    Mayonnaise, 29
  Interesting Scrambled Eggs,
    107
  Scrambled Eggs and Smoked
    Salmon, or Lox, 115
  separating, 274
  storing, 267
  Sweet Lemon Omelet, 230
  to test for freshness, 267
Emergency food
  Camper's Meal-in-One, 119
  Clam Sauce for Pasta, 183
  emergency menus, 289
  Emergency Tomato Soup, 40
  fruit and cheese, 270
  Hamburger Pie, 74
  Instant Fresh Applesauce,
    203
  Lamb or Beef with Bulgur
    Wheat (Kibbee), 68
  Quick Pasta, 270
  Quick Tomato Sauce, 184
Equipment, basic, 257–62

Forgotten Torte, 224
Freezer, stocking, 256
Fried Bread, 198
Frosting, *see* Icing
Frozen desserts, *see* Desserts,
    Ice Cream, Sherbet
Fruit
    buying and storing, 263–64
    Frozen Berry Cream, 217
    fruit salad dressing, 174
    glazed, 95, 206, 210
    Homemade Granola Fruit Bars,
        235
    pie filling, 232, 234
    preventing discoloration of,
        267
    ripening, 267
    See also individual fruits
Frying, 268

Galotsie Polonaise (Polish Stew),
    244
Garbanzo beans, *see* Chick-peas
Garlic, 19, 20
    Broccoli with Garlic and Nuts,
        124
    Chicken with Garlic (Poulet
        Béarnais), 81
    for dressing green salad, 173
    Garlic Mayonnaise (Aioli), 174
    Mashed Potatoes, 137
    peeling, 276
    sautéing, 21
Ginger, 21, 249
Glazing, 280
Graham Cracker Crust, 3, 213
Grains, 193–202
    storing, 265
    to keep on hand, 255
    See also individual grains;
        Pasta
Grapefruit
    Broiled Grapefruit, 30
Grapes
    Frozen Grapes with Yogurt,
        205

Grape and Watercress Salad,
    159
Gratiné, 280
Green beans
    "Crispy and Delicious" Green
        Beans, 131
    marinated, 133
    steamed, 121
Ground beef
    Beef and Brown Rice, 71
    Beef and Spinach, 70
    Beef with Bulgur Wheat, 68
    buying and storing, 263
    Camper's Meal-in-One, 119
    Chili Con Carne, 60
    Chinese Stir-Fried Beef, 62
    Hamburger au poivre, 64
    Hamburger Pie, 74
    Middle Eastern Hamburgers,
        59
    Spaghetti Sauce, 185
    with Peanut Sauce, 92

Ham
    Baked Ham, 53
    Chicken or Ham Salad, 167
    Cooked Grated Cabbage, 126
    Eggs with Ham or Asparagus
        in Cheese Sauce, 110
    Frittata with Ham, 108
    Ham and Melon Salad, 162
    Ham in Madeira or Red Wine,
        54
    Ham Stew, 55
    Ham Timbale, 118
    Polish Stew (Galotsie
        Polonaise), 244
    See also Prosciutto
Hamburger, *see* Ground beef
Hartshorn, 238
Herbs
    buying and storing, 19–20
    description and uses, 246–52
    dried, substituting for fresh,
        19–20
    fresh, raising and storing, 19,
        20

Olive oil, 16
  in salad dressing, 174
Omelet, Sweet Lemon, 230
One-pot dinners
  Baked Soufflé-Omelet, 116
  Beef with Brown Rice, 71
  Camper's Meal-in-One, 119
  Chicken with Sausage, 87
  Chili Con Carne, 60
  A Feast from the Oven, 243
  Ham Stew, 55
  Lamb Chops, Italian Style, 67
  Lamb or Beef with Bulgur
    Wheat (Kibbee), 68
  Polish Stew (Galotsie
    Polonaise), 244
  Sausage with Lentils, 77
Onions
  Baked Onions, 134
  Feast from the Oven, 243
  in cooking hamburger, 59
  Onion Sauce, 177
  Onion Soup, 36
  Onion Tart, 149
  peeling and cutting, 269
  preserved, 44
Oranges, 21
  Oranges in Wine, 207
Oriental noodles, 270
Oriental Sauce for Stir-Frying,
  191

Pancakes
  Cottage Cheese Pancakes, 117
Pans, see Pots and pans
Parboiling, 280
Parsley, fresh, 250
  Chinese, 248
  Italian, 250
  Pesto alla Genovese, 182
  storing, 17
Parsnip Puree, 135
Party food, see Special occasion
  dishes
Pasta
  Egg Noodles, 196

Pasta Salad, 171
  See also Sauces
Peanuts
  Peanut Sauce, 92
  West African Peanut Soup, 88
Pears
  Glazed Pears, 210
  Pears with Cointreau, 228
Peas, 15
  Green Pears in the Lebanese
    Manner (Bezela), 150
Pecans Berkeley, 226
Pepper, 22, 250
  cayenne, 154, 247
  chili, 247
  cracking, 264
  Pepper Steak (Steak au poivre),
    64
Peppers, bell (or sweet)
  Marinated Peppers, 133
  Roasted Peppers, 136
  Simmered Peppers, 151
Pesto alla Genovese, 182
Pickle juice, in salad dressing, 270
Pickles
  Corned Beef and Pickle Salad,
    161
Picnic menus, 285
Pie Crusts
  Forgotten Torte, 224
  Graham Cracker Crust, 213
  Nut Crust, 214
  Potato Pancake Crust, 140
Pie Fillings
  Chocolate Ricotta Frozen
    Dessert, 219
  Coconut Pie Filling, 233
  Strawberry Pie Filling, 234
Pies
  Hamburger Pie, 79
  Onion Tart, 149
  Ricotta Pie, 111
  Sour Apple Pie (Schnitz Pie),
    232
  testing for doneness, 268
  See also Pie Crusts, Pie
    Fillings, Quiche

Pine Nuts, 68
  Pesto alla Genovese, 182
Pineapple Sherbet, 229
Plums
  Blender Plum Soup, 45
Polenta (Cornmeal Pudding),
    197
Polish sausage
  Polish Stew, 244
  Sausage and Lentils, 77
Pork
  Chicken or Ham Salad, 167
  Chinese Stir-Fried Beef and
    Vegetables, 64
  Frittata, 108
  Polish Stew, 244
Pork Chops and Wine, 56
  Shish Kebab, 61
  Spare Ribs, 58
  Sweet and Sour Pork Chops,
    57
Potatoes
  Boiled New Potatoes, 138
    Horseradish Sauce, 179
  Broiled Potatoes, 141
  Camper's Meal-in-One, 119
  Mashed Potatoes, 137
  Potato and Onion Soup, 41
  potato baker, 260
  Potato Pancake Crust, 140
  Roman Potato Salad, 164
    in Wedding "Pie," 242
  Simple Potato Soufflé, 152
  to correct saltiness, 269
  Tomato-Potato Soup, 47
Pots and pans
  cleaning, 264
  to keep on hand, 259
Poulet Béarnais (Chicken with
    Garlic), 81
Poultry
  preparing, 265
  roasting, 266
  See also Chicken, Duck, Turkey
Prosciutto
  Ham and Melon Salad, 162
  Saltimbocca, 49

Puddings
  Cornmeal Pudding (Polenta),
    197
  Creamy Rice Pudding, 212
  Low-Cholesterol Yorkshire
    Pudding, 199
  Pumpkin Pudding, 153
  Tipsy Pudding, 231
Pumpkin Pudding, 153
Puree Soubise (Onion Sauce),
    177
Pureeing, 280

Quiche, see Timbales

Radishes
  Sautéed Red Radishes, 142
Raspberries
  Cranberry-Raspberry Ice
    Cream, 192
  Frozen Berry Cream, 217
Reducing, 280
Refrigerator, stocking, 256
Relishes
  Fresh Cranberry Relish, 192
Rice
  Beef and Brown Rice, 71
  cooking, 71
  Creamy Rice Pudding, 212
  Respectably Refurbished
    Leftover Rice, 195
  Rice Pilaf, 194
  to keep salt flowing, 264
Ricotta Pie, 111
Roux, 280
  to make White Sauce, 180

Saganaki (Fried Cheese), 112
Salads
  Apple and Beet Salad, 155
  Bulgur Wheat Salad (Tabouli),
    170
  Carrot and Turnip Salad, 165
  Carrot Salad, 157
  Chicken or Ham Salad, 167
  Chick-Pea Salad, 163
  Coleslaw, 166